LAKERS GLORY

LAKERS GLORY

FOR THE LOVE OF KOBE, MAGIC, AND MIKAN

ALAN ROSS

CUMBERLAND HOUSE
NASHVILLE, TENNESSEE

LAKERS GLORY
PUBLISHED BY CUMBERLAND HOUSE PUBLISHING, INC.
An imprint of Turner Publishing Company
Nashville, Tennessee
www.turnerbookstore.com

Cover design: Gore Studio, Inc.
Text design: John Mitchell

Editor's note: Because basketball spans two calendar years for each season played, all years given in parentheses are end dates for a particular season. For instance, the notation 1947–55 means a player started his career during the 1946 season that ended in 1947 and played through the 1954-55 season. When the word "season" appears after hyphenated years, e.g., "1971-72 season," it denotes one full season of play.

Content was compiled from a variety of sources and appears as originally presented; thus, some factual errors and differences in accounts may exist.

Library of Congress Cataloging-in-Publication Data

Ross, Alan, 1944–
Lakers glory : for the love of Kobe, Magic, and Mikan / Alan Ross.
p. cm.
Includes bibliographical references and index.
ISBN-13: 978-1-58182-554-1 (pbk. : alk. paper)
ISBN-10: 1-58182-554-4 (pbk. : alk. paper)
1. Los Angeles Lakers (Basketball team)—History. 2. Los Angeles Lakers (Basketball team)—Biography. I. Title.

GV885.52.L67R68 2006
796.323'640979494—dc22

2006032427

Printed in the United States of America

2 3 4 5 6 7 8 9 10

For Caroline

and

in memory of George Mikan

AP / Wide World Photo

George Mikan

CONTENTS

FOREWORD

As a young boy in 1952 growing up under the embryonic influence of a new medium called television, I confess to falling under its hypnotic spell. Back then, though, TV sports programming offered little to excite the imagination of an eight-year-old who had all he could handle emulating action heroes like Tom Swift Jr., the Hardy Boys, and Superman.

Yet I still recall the powerful hold a certain orange-and-blue box of cereal managed to maintain over my impressionable self when advertised on the magical little screen. The "Breakfast of Champions," it trumpeted on the outside front of its product box alongside dramatic images of major sports stars of the day—Cleveland Browns quarterback Otto Graham and golfer Sam Snead among them. It was there, through Wheaties' continuous parade of champions beckoning us to sample its flaky wares, that I was first introduced to the Lakers—the Minneapolis Lakers, that is. To the casual observer, the Lakers of that era were personified by a genuine superstar, known to all as familiarly as the names DiMaggio, Graham, Musial, and Richard were to America's other well-known pro sports. That man, a bespectacled colossus who towered over all on the hardwood floor, was already firmly established as the pinnacle power of the sport of basketball, George Mikan. And he was on that Wheaties box.

I was hooked. A pair of scissors quickly freed the great Mikan from the restraints of the cardboard cereal container, and with barely a pause to gulp down a spoonful of the Breakfast of Champions, I tucked old No. 99 inside my dungarees' back pocket, to be readily summoned and ceremoniously introduced to my school friends at the slightest whim. Only a fateful lapse resulting in an unsupervised cleansing in my mom's washing machine separated me at length from my idol. But the short-lived contact at close quarters had worked its stuff. From then on I was a Lakers fan.

It would be hard for even the mildest of hoop aficionados not to be seduced by the mystical odyssey of Lakers basketball: Mikan, Pollard, Jerry, Elgin, Wilt, Kareem, Magic, Kobe, Shaq, Riles, Phil, the great championship teams, the rock-show aura of Showtime, the star-studded fans—all interlocking into a uniquely fascinating tapestry of heroes and character, headlines and characters.

Lakers Glory is the story of the Purple & Gold (né the Blue & White) as told through the voices of its players, coaches, opponents, fans, and the media.

Inflate your Spalding, ye of Lakerdom. There's a spinning two-handed bounce pass topped by a rim-rocking reverse slam headed your way.

—A. R.

ORIGINS

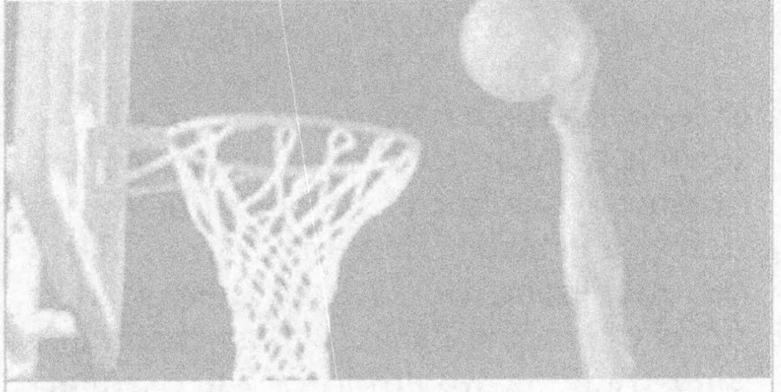

They have been alive and kicking as a franchise for the better part of six decades, briefly first in Detroit (1947), then in Minneapolis (1948–60), and finally at home in Southern California (1961–).

Tex Winter

innovator of the famed "triangle offense" and Lakers assistant coach (2000–2005)/Lakers basketball consultant (2006–)

The ultimate team in the history of the game.

Roland Lazenby
author,
on the Lakers

Pro basketball had never seen such a terrible team and wouldn't again for many seasons. Usually clubs this bad died with barely a whisper. But the Detroit Gems were different. It was from their seed of misery that the Lakers' great championship tradition would grow. Sid Hartman, a young newspaper reporter, represented a few Minneapolis businessmen who wanted to buy Maury Winston's terrible team. Better yet, they'd pay $15,000 for it.

Paul Pentecost
friend of Detroit Gems inaugural head coach Joel Mason

Fast Fact: The Gems, immediate forerunners of the Minneapolis Lakers, went 4–40 in their first and only year (1946–47) of existence, in the National Basketball League.

We were looking for a franchise. A lot of them were available. For $15,000 you could buy about anything in those days.

Sid Hartman

Minneapolis newspaper reporter/ catalyst behind the consortium that purchased the Detroit Gems in 1947, on the purchase of the Gems, an NBL franchise that became the Minneapolis Lakers the following season

The Lakers' history, with George Mikan and Vern Mikkelsen and all those guys—that really gives them a cachet, because before the Celtics started to dominate, the Lakers were a dominant team.

Kareem Abdul-Jabbar

center (1976–89)

There's a mystique surrounding the Lakers. The Lakers honestly deep down feel they will win a series and also win a necessary big game.

Steve "Snapper" Jones

nine-year ABA-NBA guard-forward/ broadcaster

Yes, he had been a four-eyed, wavy-haired goon, but before age 30, George Mikan had mastered the pro game of his time, leading his teams to seven championships in eight seasons.

Sid Hartman

Fast Fact: Mikan had propelled the Chicago American Gears to an NBL championship in 1946–1947, the year before he joined the Lakers. Mikan then led Minneapolis to six titles in seven years.

We spent more time on trains than we did at home. We knew every schedule, every porter, every dining car waiter . . .

Vern Mikkelsen

Hall of Fame forward (1950–59)

In Jim Pollard, the Lakers had a star whose superhuman, spraddle-legged flight had become almost mythical, decades before the appearance of Michael Jordan. And now, they had the King of Basketball, too, a floor-bound tank of a player, who, like Shaquille O'Neal also decades later, couldn't be stopped.

John Christgau

author,
on the Minneapolis Lakers' acquisition of superstar George Mikan to go along with Pollard during the franchise's NBL debut in the 1947–48 season

All of us could dunk except Slater Martin. But we weren't allowed to much. It was frowned on as hotdogging.

Vern Mikkelsen

It was said that the Laker attack was as imaginative as a knee in the groin: Mikan, Mikkelsen, or Pollard grabbing a rebound, tossing the ball to Slater Martin who would leisurely dribble into the forecourt as they waited for Mikan to move into the pivot.

Stew Thornley

author

FAST FACT: With no shot clock in existence before the 1954–55 season, teams like the Lakers took their time setting up shots, slowly working the ball to their big men inside.

When the Lakers and Globetrotters played, those were some tremendously competitive basketball games. You had the two great big men of that era, Mikan and Nat “Sweetwater” Clifton, playing against one another.

Bill Gleason

longtime Chicago sportswriter

FAST FACT: The world champion Minneapolis Lakers and world-renowned Harlem Globetrotters faced each other seven times between 1948 and ’52, with the ’Trotters taking the first two games, the Lakers claiming the last five. A final eighth game in 1958 was taken by Minneapolis.

We wanted to finish last. If we had traded Vern Mikkelsen, we'd have finished last. And we'd have had Bill Russell. There'd be no Los Angeles Lakers today, no Boston Celtics mystique, if we had made that deal.

Sid Hartman

on events surrounding the 1956 NBA draft. The '55 Lakers had a trade in place with Boston that likely would have netted them the No. 1 overall pick because the team's immediate performance would have suffered with the trade, but the Celtics were released from the trade commitment, and the Lakers failed to finish in last place, thereby losing their shot at the great Russell

Hey, Boomer, better check your Ouija board.

"Hot Rod" Hundley
guard (1958–63),
to forward Jim Krebs prior to boarding the team's DC-3 during a snowstorm in St. Louis following the Lakers' 135–119 loss to the Hawks, on January 17, 1960. Eerily, less than a week before, Krebs's Ouija board had predicted that the team's plane would crash. Ten minutes after takeoff, the plane's generator blew, killing the aircraft's lights, heat, and navigation system. With no radio, the pilot elected to head toward Minneapolis, climbing to 15,000 feet and attempting to steer by the stars, but ice accumulation on the plane caused it to plummet into a snow-covered cornfield in Carroll, Iowa, 150 miles off course. All escaped uninjured

There was some sadness when the Lakers left. Maybe they won too much. Maybe people took them for granted. Some people got tired of seeing them dominate completely. Until we got the Timberwolves in Minnesota, lots of people here still followed the Lakers even though they had moved to Los Angeles.

Sid Hartman

They had been averaging about 3,000 fans per game in Los Angeles. The Hawks, with Cliff Hagan, Bob Pettit, and Lenny Wilkens, had an outstanding team. The Lakers beat them in overtime. They came home to 15,000 in the Sports Arena [for Game 6]. That's when it really took off.

Chick Hearn
legendary 42-year voice of the Lakers (1961–2002), on the 1961 NBA Western Division finals

The Lakers mystique is Jerry West. He's the one constant. He's the one guy who's been there from the beginning.

Mark Heisler

longtime Los Angeles Times *columnist/author*

If Magic Johnson and David Stern got all the credit, the true architect of Hollywood Showtime was Bill Sharman, and the blueprint was the 1972 championship Lakers.

Charley Rosen

author

Jack Kent Cooke designed uniforms for both hockey and basketball. No longer did the Lakers wear their traditional blue and white. Cooke outfitted them in purple and gold, only he hated the word purple and insisted that the team call it Forum Blue.

Roland Lazenby

Central to it all is the setting, Hollywood itself, and the team's succession of playing venues—the L.A. Sports Arena, the Great Western Forum, Staples Center—the stages on which the drama has played out season after season, each building taking on the atmosphere that is a Lakers game.

Roland Lazenby

In the Forum, the Lakers wore gold, the first time in league history that the home team didn't wear white.

Roland Lazenby
on the post-1967 Lakers

AP / Wide World Photo

The Fabulous Forum

The Forum will be in essence a modern version of the greater Colosseum of ancient Rome.

Lakers 1967 press release

Fast Fact: Jack Kent Cooke once instructed his staff in a memo never to say the word "Forum" without prefacing it with the adjective "Fabulous." The Inglewood, California, facility was inaugurated on New Year's Eve 1967.

Chick Hearn's style has always been the rapid delivery, the verbal equivalent of a fast break.

Scott Ostler
Steve Springer
longtime Los Angeles Times *writers/authors, on the immortal Lakers broadcaster*

When Jerry Buss bought the team [in 1979], everything changed. You had an atmosphere like you were part of a rock and roll show.

Joe McDonnell
veteran Los Angeles sports radio personality

Jerry Buss is like a swashbuckler. He's a daredevil, a risk taker; a visionary in his own right. He's also very, very smart.

Jim Hill

Los Angeles sportscaster

All of a sudden Magic shows up, and Showtime happens. And it's real. You went into the Forum on a Friday night, and if you were a visiting team, you didn't come out of that building a winner. Everybody knew that's just how it was. It wasn't just about Magic. It wasn't just about Kareem. It was about Showtime.

Mike Wise

longtime NBA writer

It was that Showtime thing. All the stars came out at night. And the opposing team wanted to be a part of that, wanted to be involved in trying to slow that fast break down and watching Magic do his thing. It was an unbelievable atmosphere. It was like being on a stage.

Kevin Willis
twenty-year NBA forward/center

It was a beautiful time. We had graceful, beautiful players. Kareem with his skyhook. James Worthy with the floaters and finger rolls. Byron Scott with his jump shot. Michael Cooper with the way he played defense and the alley-oop for the Coop-a-Loop. Those are the things that made Showtime. And they also changed basketball.

Magic Johnson
Hall of Fame guard (1980–91, 1996)

The explosion of basketball as entertainment happened during Showtime.

Doug Krikorian

veteran Los Angeles sportswriter

In the 1980s, the Lakers had Magic Johnson, Kareem Abdul-Jabbar, and James Worthy. In the '90s and 2000, their nucleus was Shaquille O'Neal and Kobe Bryant. Both sets of superstars could take over games. They did it with offensive and defensive pressure. The Lakers have an arrogance. They force other teams to adjust to them. They don't think they can lose to you. The Celtics used to have that. The Lakers are a difficult, difficult foe. Nasty.

Steve Jones

You hate to say that getting two guys to become part of a franchise can resurrect a city, but in a big way it was part of L.A.'s healing process. The Lakers then became part of something alive.

Mike Wise

on acquiring Shaquille O'Neal from the Orlando Magic and the drafting of Kobe Bryant in 1996

For the fourth time in the franchise's illustrious half-century of history, the NBA's glamour team had managed to snare the game's most physically dominating presence by signing 24-year-old Shaquille O'Neal.

Roland Lazenby

To get this prize, I think is something that when I look back on history and the time that I've spent with this team, this might be the single most important thing we've ever done.

Jerry West

Hall of Fame guard (1961–74)/ head coach (1977–79)/ general manager (1982–2001), on the $123 million signing of Shaquille O'Neal in 1996

What the Shaq-Kobe era lacked in longevity, it made up for in entertainment value. During their last five seasons, in which they won three titles, appeared in the NBA Finals four times, and made the headlines a lot more than that, there was never anything like the Lakers—not the Charlie Finley A's or the Bronx Zoo Yankees or Da Bears or Da Bulls.

Mark Heisler

To the considerable degree that the Lakers' fate rested with Shaq and Kobe, it rested with two men who differed from each other in ways both blatant and subtle. Shaq, the self-styled big brother, was gregarious, generous, impulsive; Kobe was introspective, disciplined, measured: neither wanting a big brother nor perceiving a need for one. . . . For Shaq, success meant that he would never have to be alone; for Kobe, it meant that he would never have to be bothered. Shaq craved attention as fervently as Kobe craved privacy.

Elizabeth Kaye

author

Finally, at a ceremony in April 2002, the Los Angeles Lakers paid tribute to their origins by raising a banner with the five Minneapolis championships to the roof of Staples Sports Center. In the long overdue celebration of the franchise's Minneapolis origins, nobody seemed to notice or care that it had really been six championships.

John Christgau

on the missing Lakers title—the 1947–48 NBL crown, never officially recognized because the long-ago-defunct league was a rival to the BAA, early forerunner of the NBA. The Lakers did not join the BAA until the 1948–49 season

FAST FACT: It is hoped that one day the Lakers' media department too will give acknowledgement to the franchise's early years. The current Lakers media guide lists no members from the team's Minneapolis era on its all-time roster, not even the great Mikan or Pollard. Players with both Minneapolis and Los Angeles affiliation, like Elgin Baylor, only have their Los Angeles years recorded on the roster.

THE PURPLE & GOLD

The giant shadows strewn across the landscape of the Lakers' timeline in professional basketball aren't all the product of Mikan, Pollard, West, Baylor, Chamberlain, Magic, Kareem, Worthy, Kobe, Shaq. . . . Day in-day out components such as Brian Shaw and Hot Rod Hundley, Michael Cooper and Rudy LaRusso, Jim McMillian and Eddie Jones, the Tom Hawkinses, Ron Harpers, Rick Foxes, and Robert Horrys have all played huge roles in the attainment of Lakers glory. With large hearts often extending way beyond given abilities, their contributions are no less significant than the major stars who surrounded them.

There's the fellow that beat us. We had no way of stopping him.

Joe Lapchick

New York Knickerbockers head coach (1948–56),
on guard Whitey Skoog, shooting star of the 1953 NBA playoffs, won by the Lakers, who lost one game of the finals to New York at home before sweeping the Knicks three straight on the road for the title. Skoog's two-pointer in Game 4 was the decisive bucket in Minneapolis's 71–69 win

He was Broadway. He was Showtime before they had Showtime.

Johnny "Red" Kerr

twelve-year NBA center-forward with Syracuse, Philadelphia, and Baltimore (1955–66)/head coach with Chicago, Phoenix (1967–70), on late-'50s/early '60s guard Hot Rod Hundley

Hot Rod Hundley was talented. And hard to coach. He was a showman, always seemed to make simple plays harder than they had to be, always overdid it. He never became as good as he could have been. He didn't have the discipline. It wasn't hard to like Rod. He was young then and on a bad team with older guys who encouraged his bad habits.

John Kundla
head coach (1948–59),
on the flashy Lakers guard, the club's No. 1 draft pick in 1957

Before Pete Maravich, Rod was Pete Maravich. He did all that stuff behind the back, that razzle-dazzle stuff. Rod Hundley was great.

Red Kerr

If they were way ahead or far behind, Fred Schaus would put Hot Rod Hundley in to entertain the fans with his clowning and dribbling. When they won, Hot Rod was the sign that the game was over, like Red Auerbach lighting up his victory cigar.

Mitch Chortkoff

longtime Los Angeles sportswriter/Lakers public relations assistant in 1960

Fast Fact: The skills of Hundley, a renowned reveler in the Paul Hornung mode, diminished increasingly to the point that he was out of the NBA after six seasons, at age 27.

Dick Barnett was "Fall back, baby!" That's what he said after his shots. He'd shout it out and hold up his follow-through a little extra long. He was the only person in the NBA over six-four who couldn't stuff. Dick had some hang time, but he couldn't dunk.

John Radcliffe

longtime Lakers statistician, on the Lakers' guard-forward of the early 1960s

Rudy was good. He was a defensive player. He was the banger on the team. A guy you didn't respect sometimes during the game, a guy who did the dirty work. When it was all over, you'd say, "You know, that guy killed us." He was a hard worker, very much a background player.

Red Kerr
on '60s forward Rudy LaRusso

He came to epitomize what you wanted in a small forward. He could run the floor, post up, pass the ball; he had a nice medium-range jumper, a quick release on his shot. And he was smart.

Bill Bertka
director of scouting/former longtime assistant coach, on forward Jim McMillian, the Lakers' first-round pick in the 1970 draft from Columbia University

I always thought the Lakers' key player that season (1971–72) wasn't Jerry West or Wilt Chamberlain or Gail Goodrich. Jim McMillian was the guy, the silent difference. He didn't need the ball to be effective; he played defense, and he never missed a baseline jumper. It was McMillian who made the team's chemistry work so well.

Mike Riordan

nine-year guard with New York, Baltimore, and Washington

I really can't tell you how I fit into this team. I'm just the fat little dude wearing Number 5.

Jim McMillian

forward (1971–73), who averaged 18.8 points and 6.5 rebounds during the championship 1971–72 season as the retired Elgin Baylor's replacement

Happy Hairston's manifest affability hid a secret self that was needy and suspicious. A hustler on and off the court, Hairston also had a tendency to be shot-happy, but he always responded to a punitive benching.

Charley Rosen
on the Lakers forward from 1970 through 1975

Pat Riley's aura of arrogance helped make him a feisty over-achiever.

Charley Rosen
on the Lakers' substitute guard (1971–76) who later became head coach

I don't know anybody I ever played with that I thought was a better athlete. I mean, he could run, he could jump. He was very, very quick.

Larry Conley
former teammate of Pat Riley at Kentucky,
on the All-America Wildcat forward

Our strength has always been a well-conceived and well-executed defensive scheme, anchored by Kareem Abdul-Jabbar and complemented by "lunch-pail" guys like Jim Chones, who played on my first championship team in 1980; Kurt Rambis, who played a major role in our championships in 1982, 1985, and 1987; and A. C. Green, who started on our back-to-back championship teams in 1987 and 1988.

Magic Johnson

Years ago in L.A., our fans realized that power forward Kurt Rambis's role was as important to the Lakers' championships as mine, Kareem's, or James Worthy's role. Kurt was one of our tough guys. Scoring wasn't his primary role. His role was to be intense, to rebound; to play defense as if there was no tomorrow.

Magic Johnson

Norm Nixon would have been a star on a lot of other teams. A greyhound who could handle the ball and a great spot-up shooter, he was a fan favorite; but after Johnson arrived, no one made a fuss about Nixon.

Mark Heisler

Michael Cooper, long and lean at 6–5, was a tremendous athlete and dunker and his slams on lobs, called "Coop-a-Loops," delighted the crowd. He was high-strung and insecure, a kamikaze who'd go through a wall for a good word.

Mark Heisler

The more Michael Cooper talks trash, the better he plays.

Magic Johnson

When Michael Cooper and I go at each other during practices, it's as if it's war and our championship rings are on the line. . . . Nothing a defender can do will be tougher to handle than what Coop's already thrown at me.

Magic Johnson

He was so invaluable. Coop would come in for a few minutes and really change everything in a game.

Kareem Abdul-Jabbar

Hall of Fame center (1976–89), on guard-forward and defensive specialist Michael Cooper

Kobe calls me the youngest "old head" he knows. He says I have too much energy for an old guy.

A. C. Green

forward (1986–93, 2000)

The Lakers had a rookie center from Yugoslavia named Vlade Divac, who had it all except American-playground toughness.

Mark Heisler
on the team's 6–11 center from 1990 through '96 plus an encore season in 2005

If you find a guy with a passion to win, you got yourself something special. Nick Van Exel was very passionate. He wanted to win badly and got frustrated when he didn't.

Larry Drew
former assistant coach

The Lakers gave me a lot of confidence to be the leader, and it was a role I wanted.

Nick Van Exel
guard (1994–98)

Eddie Jones has been more than we ever could ask for. He doesn't have one negative attribute. And there's not a lot of players you can say that about in the NBA.

Jerry West
on the 6–6, 190-pound guard/ forward from 1995 through 1999

Glen Rice is a guy who always seems to have nine lives. He keeps coming back all the time.

Phil Jackson
on the former Lakers forward (1999–2000)

Veteran role players Rick Fox, Ron Harper, Derek Fisher, Brian Shaw, and Robert Horry would weigh large as a factor in the team's ability to win three straight titles.

Roland Lazenby
on Kobe and Shaq's supporting cast for the 2000–02 championship run

Robert Horry was basketball's Reggie Jackson, the Mr. June to Jackson's Mr. October.

Elizabeth Kaye

That puts him up there with all the clutch people you would name—Reggie Miller, Jerry West.

Brian Shaw
guard (2000–03),
on last-shot master Robert Horry

Fast Fact: Horry canned three dramatic three-pointers to produce Lakers wins in the 2001 playoffs: a first-round series-ending trey against Portland with 2.1 seconds remaining; a three with 56 seconds left that pushed the Lakers' lead to seven in the elimination of Sacramento in the Western Conference semifinals; and a Game 3 three-pointer against Philadelphia with 47 seconds left, putting L.A. up two games to one in their eventual NBA Finals triumph over the Sixers. Horry struck again with two three-pointers in the final minute and 39 seconds of Game 4 of the 2002 Western Conference finals, the final one coming as time expired, for a 100–99 Lakers win that evened the series at two games apiece.

Since I started coaching in 1989, I can't think of a player, except for Michael Jordan and maybe Reggie Miller, who has nailed more clutch shots.

Phil Jackson
on Robert Horry

I guess I've always been able to hit shots because I don't care if I miss or make it. A lot of guys put so much pressure on themselves to make shots in the end. But with me, I'm like, "If I make it, I make it, if I don't, I don't." But I don't worry about it, because there are always more important things in life.

Robert Horry
forward (1997–2003)

As a product of North Carolina, Rick Fox had been coached by the mythic Dean Smith, who was coached by Phog Allen, who learned the game from basketball's inventor James Naismith.

Elizabeth Kaye

Harp was the guy who could jump on a bike careening down a hill and steady it.

Kurt Rambis

center-forward (1982–88, 1994–95), head coach (1999)/assistant coach (2001–),
on guard-forward Ron Harper (2000–01), termed the Lakers' "insurance policy" by Phil Jackson

When he plays under control, utilizing his raw skills—on our team, only Kobe is a better all-around athlete—he becomes a huge weapon for us.

Phil Jackson

on Devean George, the team's No. 1 pick in the 1998 NBA draft, from tiny Augsburg (Minn.) College

He's been doing the defensive part all year long. Sometimes, the people want more. Tonight he gave them more.

Kobe Bryant

guard (1997–),
on teammate Kwame Brown's 21-point, 12-rebound performance in the Lakers' 87–80 victory over Sacramento, March 22, 2006, to move L.A. into seventh place in the Western Conference

The guy's got the best body in the NBA. He's got to throw it around a little bit.

Lamar Odom

forward (2005–),
on 6–11, 270-pound center Kwame Brown

LAKERS CHARACTER

He'd rather practice than take a day off.

Jerry West
on Magic Johnson

It has never mattered to me who got the job done as long as it got done, even if it's not me.

Magic Johnson

George Mikan and I were always very critical of each other, very frank. But that helped our relationship, because nothing festered. We always got it off our chests.

Jim Pollard
Hall of Fame forward (1948–55)

There are three keys to winning basketball games: defense, defense, defense.

Magic Johnson

What we established in the '80s—what we took over from Jerry West and Wilt in '72—is that winning attitude. That's what L.A. is about.

Michael Cooper
guard/forward (1979–90)

Winning is winning, and to be a leader you have to understand that winning is more important than being the star.

Magic Johnson

The closer you get to the magic circle, the more enticing it becomes. It's like a drug. It's seductive because it's always there, and the desire is always there to win one more game. There's no question with me. . . . I was obsessed with winning.

Jerry West
who reached the NBA finals seven times and lost all seven times, six times to Boston, before finally grabbing the coveted championship in 1972, thanks to an MVP performance for the ages from center Wilt Chamberlain. In all, West's Lakers lost eight of nine NBA Finals

Byron Scott told me how important it is during the season to keep up your work habits. At this level, you always have to be working to improve your game or you'll get left behind.

Kobe Bryant

No player worked harder, especially telling when you consider that few players were graced with such talent. Kobe worked no matter what. He worked through injury, through adversity, through those difficult first seasons when it was not certain that he would measure up to the off-the-charts hype that greeted his early entry into the league.

Elizabeth Kaye

Playing hard is the ultimate respect.

Magic Johnson

Derek Fisher was a genuine leader, a voice of faith and hope. The team had never been more in need of what he brought to the game: the hustle, the grit, the all-out effort, the heart.

Phil Jackson

on the L.A. guard's return late in the 2001 season after missing 62 games. In his first game back, Fisher netted a career-high 26 points and recorded eight assists and six steals in a win over Boston

You have to really want to play defense. You have to really want to double team, rotate to the open man, and pressure your man for the length of the floor. Defense is truly the thinking man's side of the game.

Magic Johnson

I feel weird going out (doing the club scene) on the road, knowing that you have a game the next night. That's not handling your business.

Kobe Bryant

As a kid he had played until he vomited, then kept playing until he hit the wall. Still he played. And it taught him that you can push yourself beyond the point where your body shuts down, and from that he deduced that the game was mental, that mind could win out over matter. Too much of the time the game was too easy for him. . . . For Kobe there were no obstacles; there were only challenges.

Elizabeth Kaye

During the streak, none of the guys showed any kind of big ego. Not even Wilt. We were pulling for each other.

Flynn Robinson
guard (1972–73),
on the Lakers' untouchable winning streak for the ages: the 33 straight wins logged during the 1971–72 championship season

I coached against Karl Malone for about 15 years, but it wasn't until I started observing him day after day on the practice floor and in the weight room that I fully appreciated the extent of his dedication.

Phil Jackson
head coach (2000–04, 2006–),
on the 18-year Utah Jazz power forward who came to L.A. in 2004 in search of a championship ring

Never underestimate the value of a little respect.

Magic Johnson

LAKERS HUMOR

There was the night that Elgin Baylor got 71 points in Madison Square Garden. Hot Rod Hundley got in a cab that night after the game and told the driver, "Me and Elgin got 78 points tonight."

Red Kerr

Jim Pollard, Vern Mikkelsen, and George Mikan. People used to say that you could get two ushers to play with them, and you could still make the playoffs.

Red Kerr

At West Virginia as a freshman, Hot Rod Hundley had the chance to break the school scoring record. He needed two more points, and he was at the free-throw line. He threw up hook shots. Asked about it later, he said, "If I broke the record as a freshman what would I have to look forward to as a sophomore?"

Red Kerr

In his first pro game during the 1957–58 season, rookie forward McCoy Ingram, a six-foot jumping jack, got the ball after a jump ball and promptly shot it into the opponent's goal.

Roland Lazenby

K. C. Jones used to tackle Jerry West rather than let him get off a jump shot.

Fred Schaus
head coach (1961–67)

The world is made up of Davids, and I am Goliath.

Wilt Chamberlain
center (1969–73)

Jerry West declined. He'd sooner jump into a pile of snakes before a dressing room.

Mark Heisler
on West being asked by Lakers owner Jerry Buss to coach the team a second time in 1982

Jack Kent Cooke should fork up the money to go test Happy Hairston for color blindness.

Chick Hearn
after the former Lakers forward once inbounded the ball directly to the other team

My attitude towards Shaq's struggles at the line has evolved. Early on I twitched so nervously on the bench—"Gosh, he's going to miss his free throws and it's really going to hurt us!"—that I probably wore a hole in my pants. These days I assume he's going to miss them, and when he proves me wrong, I consider the points to be a bonus.

Phil Jackson

Tell me when we reach 44. That's how many consecutive games my volleyball team won last summer.

Wilt Chamberlain

during the Lakers' record-setting 33-game winning streak in the 1971–72 season

He wears contact lenses on the court, horned rims off the court, and might be accused of being Clark Kent, except that he could never fit into a phone booth to change clothes.

Frank Deford
Sports Illustrated *writer, on Pat Riley, the player*

Chick Hearn was riding up a hotel elevator when it stopped and a man got on wearing a Superman costume. The man rode up one story and got out. "Silly son of a bitch could've jumped that high," Hearn whispered indignantly.

Scott Ostler
Steve Springer

LAKERS LEGENDS

The athletic feats of the Kangaroo Kid became the stuff of Minnesota legend. Like Superman, Jim Pollard could leap tall buildings in a single bound. Playing baseball in the summer in the small town of Jordan, Minn., his monster home runs were too long to be measured, and after one bounced into the boxcar of a passing freight train, observers joked that he had hit a home run in Minnesota that landed in Missouri. . . . When he died in 1993 in Stockton, California, at the age of 70, he stood as a giant in talent and basketball history.

John Christgau

AP / WIDE WORLD PHOTO

Jim Pollard

At six-foot-six (he would always list his official height at 6–3), Jim Pollard was a rare bird in 1940s basketball. He could run and jump and dunk and dribble and pass. He could even execute a reverse jam. No one envisioned a midair slam dance in 1947. But he could play above the rim. Many of the players in this whites-only era were mechanical, one- and two-dimensional athletes. Not Pollard. He was a prototype for the future. Sid Hartman would later compare him to Michael Jordan, but Pollard actually was more like Scottie Pippen. He was a terror from the wing. The fans called him "the Kangaroo Kid." Later, Billy Cunningham would earn the nickname, but Pollard was the original.

Roland Lazenby

If Jim Pollard had played in the modern NBA, he would have been a big point guard, like a Magic Johnson.

John Kundla

Those three big bastards made every court look narrow. Mikkelsen was a brute.

Paul Seymour

Syracuse Nationals forward (1948–60), on the 1950–54 Minneapolis front line of 6–10 center George Mikan, 6–4 forward Jim Pollard, and 6–7 forward Vern Mikkelsen

Vern Mikkelsen was the workhorse. He was the guy that took the tough defensive player, rebounded well, was a hard body under the basket. He reminded me of what Dennis Rodman was to the Bulls, what Rodman was to Michael Jordan and Scottie Pippen. The guy who did the work, the offensive rebounding.

Red Kerr

Slater Martin, the high-scoring college player at Texas, became a low-scoring, ball-distributing pro guard, running the Lakers' lumbering offense. Later, after helping the Lakers to four championships, Martin would move on to the St. Louis Hawks and direct them to yet another title, accomplishments that landed him in the Hall of Fame.

Roland Lazenby

Slater Martin would never take a shot unless it was an absolute necessity. Nevertheless, he hit .410 from the floor that season, eighth best in the league, an indication of just how many long set shots those old-timers took.

Roland Lazenby
on the 5–10 point guard's 10.6 scoring average for the 1952–53 season

With his exceptional driving ability and twisting, driving layups, in which he often changed direction in mid-air, Elgin Baylor caused the terms "body control" and "hang time" to become part of basketball lexicon.

Stew Thornley

Elgin was very strong. He would get bumped all the time, but it never seemed to throw him off stride. Even in the air, he would get bumped a lot, but his concentration was so good that the shot would still go where he wanted it to go. He used the glass a lot. I never saw him dunk. It wasn't the thing to do in those days.

John Radcliffe

He delighted in taking the unusual shot. He seemed to feel he was cheating if he could see the basket when he shot, much less be facing it. His pet play was one in which he drove across the key, past the basket, then twisted up and spun the ball backwards toward the basket, exerting "English" like Minnesota Fats caroming one into a corner pocket.

Bill Libby
author,
on the moves of Elgin Baylor

Elgin Baylor was just a machine.

Satch Sanders
thirteen-year Boston Celtics forward

Most of the time, I never knew what I was going to do until I did it. Sometimes when the ball went in, I couldn't believe it myself.

Elgin Baylor
Hall of Fame forward (1959–72), who once scored 71 points in a game and posted 61 points in a playoff game

Elgin Baylor was so spectacular he could sell tickets with the way he played.

Mitch Chortkoff

AP / Wide World Photo

Elgin Baylor

It was an honor to play with him. I never considered Elgin Baylor as someone I competed against. He is without a doubt one of the truly great players to play this game. I hear people talking about great players today, and I don't see many that compare to him. He had that wonderful, magical instinct for making plays, for doing things that you just had to watch. I learned from him, from watching him. I had an appreciation for other people's talents. It was incredible to watch Elgin play.

Jerry West

Elgin was a shorter version of Karl Malone. He had a lot of power.

Rod Hundley

Elgin Baylor's father named him on an impulse after his treasured pocket watch.

Bill Libby

Without reservation Elgin Baylor is the greatest cornerman who ever played pro basketball.

Fred Schaus

Jerry West came to L.A. in 1960 with a flattop haircut, skinny legs, and a high-pitched mountain twang, like he had just fallen off the turnip truck. Bumpkin personified. It was the age of TV's *Beverly Hillbillies*, and the shy, serious country boy found a Hollywood eager to lampoon him. Elgin Baylor came up with the name "Zeke from Cabin Creek." West wasn't even from Cabin Creek. He hated that name.

Roland Lazenby

I thought he was sensational. He was so cooperative from a coach's standpoint. Anything you wanted to do, he'd go along with it or make suggestions. You couldn't ask for a better player, especially being a superstar.

Bill Sharman
head coach (1972–76),
on Jerry West

I hated to guard him because of his quickness. I'd rather guard Oscar Robertson, because Oscar just backed you down and beat you with strength. But Jerry West embarrassed you. He was one of the first players that had tremendous, tremendous quickness but also could take the ball over the rim. Plus he was a great defensive player.

Kevin Loughery
eleven-year NBA guard
with Detroit, Baltimore,
and Philadelphia

Jerry West was totally unselfish. He was so fundamentally sound that he'd throw two-handed bounce passes. With his long arms and his flawless decision making, West was absolutely the most important guy on the team.

Dr. Jack Ramsay
twenty-one-year NBA coach/
broadcaster

AP / Wide World Photo

Jerry West

He is the master. They can talk about the others, build them up, but he is the one. He is the only guard.

Larry Siegfried

seven-year Boston Celtics guard, on Jerry West, after the Lakers standout was named NBA Finals MVP in 1969, the first and only time a player from a losing team has gained the honor

I had nights where you just couldn't guard me. I was making them from everywhere. If I made it from the outside, it was an impossible task for the defensive player to guard me. Quickness and the ability to draw fouls is an art.

Jerry West

We had a rule whenever we wound up with a two-on-one advantage against Jerry West. West had such long arms that it was impossible to pass the ball anywhere near him without him reaching out and getting a piece of it. You always had to take it to the hole yourself. The Lakers had the total package on both ends of the court.

Jack Marin
eleven-year NBA forward with Baltimore, Houston, Buffalo, and Chicago

I felt that I was gifted enough to do some things on the basketball floor. I couldn't do everything I wanted to do, because if that was the case, I'd have won every game.

Wilt Chamberlain

Wilt is absolutely awesome. He's my all-time most valuable player.

Billy Cunningham
nine-year Hall of Fame forward, and later, eight-year head coach of the Philadelphia 76ers

Scoring 50 points a night was just an average night's work for Wilt. Afterwards, he'd stroll off the court, drink a half gallon of milk, and take a cab back to his hotel. Then he'd have a T-bone steak, french fries, and about a half dozen bottles of soda while he watched TV. I don't think there will ever be anyone quite like him again.

Frank McGuire
longtime college head coach/ Philadelphia Warriors head coach (1962), on Wilt Chamberlain

Fast Fact: During the 1961–62 season, Chamberlain, incredibly, set an NBA record with Philadelphia that will likely stand for all time, when he averaged 50.4 points a game.

Wilt Chamberlain was . . . flamboyant and unpredictable, blessed with colossal talents and appetites. None of his teammates dared to challenge the sheer power and magnitude of Chamberlain's ego—and they were grateful for the playful benevolence with which he regarded mere humans such as them.

Charley Rosen

Chamberlain was a megalomaniac, if a fun one.

Mark Heisler
on the grandiose Stilt

Most people couldn't relate to what an imposing physical thing Wilt was. The first time you see him, it's like you're standing in his shadow. He's so big. Then he was really smart and a great athlete.

Bill Russell
Boston Celtics 13-year
Hall of Fame center

AP / WIDE WORLD PHOTO

Wilt Chamberlain

Wilt was my greatest opponent. It's not even close.

Bill Russell

A powerhouse guy. Could do everything. Shoot, rebound, block shots, passes. He led the league in assists one year. That's the incredible stat. No center's ever done that.

Dr. Jack Ramsay
on Wilt Chamberlain

I just liked Wilt. There was the size factor and what he could do. He could shoot, rebound, and pass. People always focus on his scoring, but they forget that he also led the league in assists and rebounds. Wilt could do what he wanted. In trying to do everything well, I really tried to imitate him.

Magic Johnson

Gail Goodrich was a great player. He was about six-two, six-three, but he had arms down to his toes. He had that seven-foot wingspan. He could go to the basket because of that and take it over the rim. He was a very good post-up player, and very cocky. He believed in himself.

Kevin Loughery

They called Gail Goodrich "Stumpy." He was only about six feet, but he had the longest arms in the NBA. He was left-handed and fearless going to the basket. He would disappear into a crowd of big men; then suddenly the ball would kiss off the glass and fall in.

John Radcliffe

Stumpy knows how to set a man up. Why, he'd drive on anybody—Russell, Jabbar, or even Wilt. Hell, he's such a great competitor he'd even drive on King Kong.

K. C. Jones
Boston Celtics Hall of Fame guard/head coach with four NBA teams/Lakers assistant coach under Bill Sharman, on Gail Goodrich

Kareem Abdul-Jabbar, that first year Jerry West coached him, was as good a player as this league has ever had. You talk about a dominant center. People forget. He single-handedly beat the Golden State Warriors in a series that went seven games (1977). People could not stop Kareem.

Doug Krikorian

Magic baptized him. He transformed him into an enthusiastic player.

Paul Westhead

head coach (1980–82), on the dour Kareem Abdul-Jabbar, who had always had a contentious relationship with the media prior to Magic Johnson's arrival in L.A. for the 1979–80 season

For us, everything revolved around Kareem Abdul-Jabbar from the moment I arrived for my first training camp in 1979 until the 1986–87 season, when Pat Riley restructured our attack and focused most of it around me. As the team's point guard, I almost always had the basketball, but the screens, the cuts, the openings, they all keyed on Kareem. He was our anchor during my first ten seasons.

Magic Johnson

He defies logic. He's the most unique and durable athlete of our time, the best you'll ever see.

Pat Riley
head coach (1982–90), on Kareem Abdul-Jabbar

Kareem often chafed under the burden of greatness. He resented the media for their expectations and their preoccupation with one man in a five-man game. His aloofness with the press and the public made him an easy target for criticism.

Scott Ostler
Steve Springer

He has the art of keeping the world at arm's length down to a bittersweet science. He may be quoted less than any major athlete at the top of his profession. He himself admits to a "mysterious" public image.

Scott Ostler
Steve Springer
on Kareem Abdul-Jabbar

Kareem Abdul-Jabbar always said that there was no secret to his longevity. He always credited his yoga. To Kareem, stretching was as important as any other part of practice. He was so confident in his system that he didn't even tape his ankles, something every other player in the league does as a way of preventing ankle injuries.

Magic Johnson

Kareem would save me a seat next to him on airplanes and buses. Everyone else would be talking hoops all the time. We would talk religion, or politics, or horses. He could talk about anything. He's the most well-read person I've ever met.

Brad Holland

guard (1980–81)

AP / Wide World Photo

Kareem Abdul-Jabbar

Kareem is just a nice guy, a very intelligent guy. I found him to be very open. He has a lot of insight, a lot of wisdom.

Jim Brewer
forward (1981–82)

At the end of the game, he's the best.

Wilt Chamberlain
on Kareem Abdul-Jabbar

Abdul-Jabbar is the best scoring machine ever put together.

Dick Motta
twenty-five-year NBA head coach

No sports figure has ever made as many encores as Kareem Abdul-Jabbar. Every year he is supposed to be the old man, ready to surrender to the new fast gun in town. And every year he shoots 'em down. It was supposed to be the Ralph Sampson Era, the Akeem Olajuwon Era, the Patrick Ewing Era. But at age 29, Abdul-Jabbar is still living the Kareem Era.

Scott Ostler
Steve Springer

It's as if I have survived the whole cycle, life and death, and here I still am.

Kareem Abdul-Jabbar
reflecting on his life, at 38, following the Lakers' NBA Finals win over Boston in 1985, in which he was named playoffs MVP. Jabbar to that time had withstood the murder in 1973 of seven Muslim friends in a Washington, D.C., townhouse that he had purchased for orthodox Muslim leader Hamaas Abdul-Khaalis; a stormy relationship with the pro basketball press and NBA fans throughout his Milwaukee Bucks years; and the loss of his Bel-Air mansion in a 1983 fire

No disrespect to Bill Russell or Wilt, but Kareem will go down as the greatest player ever.

Pat Riley

He was still a freshman at Michigan State when I first saw him play. Here was this 6–9 kid with a big man's body, well over 200 pounds, playing what was essentially a little man's game. He was the size of most college centers, but he was playing point guard for his team. He was the floor leader, calling all the plays and moving everybody around the floor like an orchestra leader. He was handling the ball like a six-footer, like it was an extension of his hand. He was absolutely in complete command.

Jerry West

on Earvin "Magic" Johnson

Basketball is my life. It's what I love. It's my escape. There's no substitute for being on the court.

Magic Johnson

He was making the kind of moves I'd never seen from a player his size. He was dribbling the length of the floor, looking one way and passing another. He was hitting every open man, making all the right decisions. Basically, he was controlling the entire game. He was their unmistakable leader. I was astounded.

Jerry West
on 6–9 Michigan State freshman point guard Earvin Johnson Jr.

The dramatic difference was Magic. He just had so many skills that we didn't have and were crucial to the success of any team. . . . Magic did so many things in a combination, the effect was amazing. He just changed everybody's attitude.

Kareem Abdul-Jabbar

AP / WIDE WORLD PHOTO

Magic Johnson

Magic's got a star in Hollywood, and they had no choice but to give it to him because he's the most famous star in all of Los Angeles. Period.

John Salley
forward/center (2000)

Only a handful of players like Magic—guys like Larry Bird and Michael Jordan—have that special ability to make those around them better.

Jerry West

Magic is a great, great basketball player. The best I've ever seen.

Larry Bird
Boston Celtics Hall of Fame forward and Johnson's main career rival

He was as big as Bill Russell, as smart and creative as Tiny Archibald, and as exciting as Bob Cousy.

Jerry West
on Magic Johnson

There were nine or ten points gone from my game just from his passing ability, just from his getting the ball to you in unique situations. His leadership qualities were unique. Here's a guy who didn't mind getting on you. Some guys can do that; most can't. Plus Earvin had energy all the time. Energy at shootaround, energy on the bus, energy in the locker room, energy while he slept. He would not let you down. He would not let his team lose.

James Worthy
forward (1983–94),
on Magic Johnson, after the Lakers superstar point guard prematurely retired from the game following the 1991 season after testing positive for HIV

Magic was my favorite player as a kid, besides my dad, of course. I tried to do all the stuff he was doing back in those days. I loved the way Magic got everybody involved in the game—his teammates, fans, everybody.

Kobe Bryant

James Worthy was the next big six-nine player who played like a six-two player. Nobody had seen that. He redefined that 3 spot. Here he was a power forward now playing a 3 position and every now and then he could slide to the 2 spot. That's what made it unique: that he could still have that power forward mentality to get down in the low post and get it done.

Michael Cooper
guard (1979–90)

I used to tell Patrick Ewing, "Once this kid learns how to score over the top with a jump hook or turnaround jumper, you can shut it down, because the game's over. Back in Orlando, he had to get beside you or around you to dunk it. He was limited by that. But once he learned to score over the top, you could forget it. You couldn't play him. He's too agile.

Herb Williams
eighteen-year NBA center-forward with Indiana, Dallas, New York Knicks, and Toronto, on Shaquille O'Neal

Clearly, if the offense doesn't run through me, the house doesn't get guarded. Period.

Shaquille O'Neal
center (1997–2004)

We're built on the fact that Kobe and Shaq are the best one-two combination in the game, and the complementary players around them want to play as a team and want to figure in this.

Phil Jackson
during 2000–01

He was a better leader than I was informed. Maybe that was because he was young. Perhaps it was a function of maturing, but he was a nice leader on our team.

Del Harris
head coach (1995–99), on Shaquille O'Neal

A guy his size, as mobile as he is, it's almost unfair.

Herb Williams
on Shaquille O'Neal

When I was first coming up, my father always said, "Be like Wilt, be like Kareem, be like Hakeem." That's why I am who I am today. It's because I had people to look up to.

Shaquille O'Neal

He's the most dominating player in our league. He's powerful, strong, able to get the ball in the hole. He's improved immensely, starting to make shots further from the basket. He's just so dominating that they have an opportunity here to do something great for a number of years.

Larry Bird

Indiana Pacers head coach, on Finals MVP Shaquille O'Neal following the Pacers' 4–1 loss to L.A. in the 2000 NBA Finals

AP / Wide World Photo

Shaquille O'Neal

From now on, I am no longer "The Big Aristotle." I want to be known as "The Big Shakespeare," because it was Shakespeare who said, "Some men are born great, some achieve greatness, and some have greatness thrust upon them."

Shaquille O'Neal
after L.A. won the 2000 NBA championship and O'Neal copped the first of three straight NBA Finals MVP awards

I see an analogy between Shaq and a 1972 220SL Mercedes. In 2004 one is not going to race this car at 100 miles per hour down Sunset Boulevard because it would risk damaging the vehicle. How many times do you expect Shaq to run up and down the floor before something goes wrong?

Phil Jackson

If I'm on a team where we come down and call plays every time, then it's time for me to quit. Then I'm not gonna be an effective big man no more. I don't want to play like that. I want to run and get crazy and look at the fans and make faces.

Shaquille O'Neal

He gave everything for me and the Lakers when it really mattered. I took this job for the opportunity to coach him, and he made it an experience I will cherish forever.

Phil Jackson
on Shaquille O'Neal

For all his bravado, Shaq is a very sensitive, fragile soul who appreciates any sign of tenderness. He's often maligned for his lack of durability, his unwillingness to play with severe physical discomfort, yet critics have no clue to what he must regularly overcome to compete at this level. Nobody can begin to understand what it must feel like to haul a 340-pound body around, stopping and starting, stopping and starting.

Phil Jackson

Nobody in the NBA can defend him.

Phil Jackson
on Shaquille O'Neal

This guy's special. He's very special even though he's a high school player.

Bill Bertka

on 17-year-old phenom Kobe Bryant's workout for the Lakers prior to the 1996 NBA draft

From day one he knew the things he wanted to accomplish in his career. Because of his talent level, it's almost like a self-fulfilling prophecy for him.

Derek Fisher

guard (1997–2004), on Kobe Bryant

It's not arrogance. It's not his personality. He's not a selfish person. He's not a guy that only thinks of himself. He's just a guy who has an immeasurable amount of confidence in his ability to play the game.

Derek Fisher

on Kobe

I don't want to sound blasphemous, but he really can be like Michael Jordan.

Jerry Reynolds

Sacramento Kings director of player personnel, on Kobe Bryant, during the 1997–98 season

He's got a level of commitment to his game and to wanting to be the best that few guys have. Nobody on our team has that commitment, that's for sure.

Scott Skiles

former Phoenix Suns head coach, on Kobe Bryant during the 2000–01 season

His enthusiasm infuses this basketball club. He's got the energy, the drive, the moxie, and also a feel, an uncanny instinctual feel for this basketball game.

Phil Jackson

on six-time NBA All-Defensive Team selectee Kobe Bryant

The first thing about Kobe Bryant is that his talent is astounding. The second thing is his body exaggerates that talent with his height and his length. The third thing is he has the uncommon will to win. It's the same exact will to win as Michael Jordan.

Gregg Popovich
San Antonio Spurs head coach

Kobe is the only player we ever saw who had the same level of competitiveness as Michael. No one else is even close.

Phil Jackson staff member

Jerry West and Kobe Bryant had strong similarities in their respective games: the brilliant shooting, the rabid defense, the focus, the will to win, and the need to adjust to a dominant center.

Elizabeth Kaye

I don't really think about my image. It will shake out. People who talk about me in a negative manner, they don't know me. If they had a chance to be around me, kick it with me or whatever and get to know me, then they could judge. I think that will come out as the years go by. People will see how I really am, what I'm really about.

Kobe Bryant

He's the best all-around player in the league, the best scorer, the best competitor, and the one guy who terrifies everyone else.

Bill Simmons
ESPN.com
on Kobe

He was 22 and viewed by many as the "Air Apparent" to Michael Jordan, though their games were very different. He was an off-the-dribble player, handling the ball, creating—while at the same age Jordan got the ball more often than not when he was in a position to shoot it. In any case, he did not want to be the second Michael Jordan. He wanted to be the first Kobe Bryant, the greatest ever to play the game.

Elizabeth Kaye

It's like God put Kobe down here for us to watch him play basketball.

Lamar Odom

AP / Wide World Photo

Kobe Bryant

"I was like a computer," he told *Sports Illustrated*'s Ian Thomsen early on. "I retrieved information to benefit my game." He didn't play on a team or learn street moves like the crossover dribble until he came back to the States for high school. This meant that his path to the NBA was devoid of the usual gyms and playgrounds—even, for the most part, of teammates. Thomsen came to think of Kobe as the NBA's first test-tube player.

Elizabeth Kaye

You know what? You're my idol.

Shaquille O'Neal
to Kobe Bryant, following Bryant's 45-point explosion that dominated L.A.'s 104–90 victory over San Antonio in Game 1 of the 2001 Western Conference finals

Michael Jordan never played like Kobe. He never tried to play like that. Michael let the game come to him a lot more. Kobe is going to take it to the game.

Tex Winter

former Chicago Bulls/L.A. Lakers assistant coach,
on Kobe Bryant's 35.0-point average at the 2006 all-star break, the highest since Michael Jordan's 37.0 average before the break 19 years ago

Basically, he's Elvis and everyone else is Joe Esposito.

Bill Simmons

on Kobe Bryant

Fast Fact: Esposito, from 1960–77, was Presley's aide, road manager, and confidante.

When remembering the 2005–06 season 10 years from now, which player will pop into your head first? Answer: Kobe. The dude scored 62 in three quarters against Dallas, then 81 against Toronto a few weeks later. He's about to become the fifth player in NBA history to average 35 points a game (along with Wilt, MJ, Elgin, and Rick Barry). He made up with Shaq. He made up with Phil. He made up with Nike. He appeared on the cover of *Slam Magazine* with a mamba snake wrapped around him. He did everything but make the obligatory cameo on *Will and Grace*.

Bill Simmons

He has become "Must-See-TV." Alone, win or lose, Kobe Bryant has made it essential that we not miss him play a game of basketball this season. . . . For better or worse, richer or broke, wins or losses, it made you want to pay attention to what may happen next in the Book of Kobe.

Scoop Jackson
ESPN.com
following Kobe's 81-point outburst against Toronto, January 22, 2006

Kobe is the next Kobe Bryant.

John Salley

LEGENDARY COACHES

An acrobatic dunk will make it onto SportsCenter. A simple, unspectacular bounce pass in the rhythm of the offense will not. System basketball has been replaced by players who want to be the system.

Phil Jackson

John Kundla gets no recognition. He did a great job of molding the team, taking care of the players' idiosyncrasies.

George Mikan

on the Lakers' championship head coach of the late 1940s–1950s

FAST FACT: Minneapolis head coach Kundla was the Phil Jackson of his day as a coach/motivator/psychologist/peacemaker, while guiding the team to six titles.

He did his job, and he did it well. Everybody thought it was easy because he had a talented team. It's not easy to have those guys and win and keep your senses.

Paul Seymour

on Minneapolis Lakers head coach John Kundla

Most of our players responded very positively to Fred Schaus early on. Obviously, later in their careers, when a coach has been around a few years, the players have heard all of his stories. Frankly, it wears out. He did a very competent job with our team. We played hard all the time, and I think that's a tribute to the coach.

Jerry West

I would have loved to shove that victory cigar down Red Auerbach's throat. We came awfully close to putting that damn thing out.

Fred Schaus

Butch van Breda Kolff was just all over the place. It was amazing how he would just throw himself down on the seats. The body language alone was enough to get him technicals.

John Radcliffe
on the Lakers' head coach in 1968 and '69

I was intrigued by Bill Sharman. He had that inner intensity. I later saw the same quality in Joe Gibbs [who coached Cooke's Washington Redskins to three Super Bowl championships].

Jack Kent Cooke
owner (1965–79)

You had the strongest personality in Bill Sharman. He was on fire right at that time. He was at the peak of his career with his personal intensity as a coach. He was a great communicator. No frills. No bullshit. With Bill, it was all down to productivity.

Bill Bertka

on the Lakers' coach during their 1971–72 world championship season

It was difficult for us to relate to him in the beginning, because he was covered with Boston green. But in time we came around. He was a low-key guy, but very competitive, very feisty.

Pat Riley

on the Lakers' new head coach in 1971, former Boston Celtics Hall of Fame forward Bill Sharman

Players often grumbled, but Bill Sharman's game-day shootaround soon became a staple of NBA preparation. So would his notions on diet and exercise. He required his players to become students of the game. His Lakers were the first NBA team to break down game film and study it as football coaches did.

Roland Lazenby
on the Lakers coach's innovations, introduced in 1971

Bill Sharman's introduction of the morning shootaround revolutionized basketball. After the Lakers won (in '72), every team in the league followed suit. The result was that come game time players were sharper and teams were better prepared. Bill brought a new sense of discipline and organization to the NBA that significantly upgraded the quality of play.

Phil Jackson

With Jerry, there was something in the atmosphere that became infectious. Everybody wanted to feel about the team the way Jerry did. He was never arrogant. He had great intuition. He wanted to see what each of us could do. When you get that kind of atmosphere going, it does something to bring you near the top of your skills.

Kareem Abdul-Jabbar

on Jerry West's inaugural season (1976–77) as head coach

He was never a person to seek adulation. Even as a general manager he downplayed himself. But he was driven for it, driven for greatness; his drive greater than his fear of not succeeding. He's never been one to sing his own praises, to laud himself.

Pete Newell
former head coach at the University of San Francisco, Michigan State, and Cal-Berkeley, on onetime Lakers star guard, head coach, and general manager Jerry West

As I moved into the NBA, I was lucky enough to find myself being coached by Jack McKinney. He didn't try to make the players do things they couldn't do just for the sake of some theory.

Magic Johnson

Jack took all our skills and developed the perfect system for us. . . . He knew we could run, and he didn't mind giving us the freedom to run every chance we got.

Magic Johnson
on Jack McKinney (1980)

I'm not searching for the meaning of life in the NBA. But it gives me a feeling of being totally alive every time I'm out on the floor.

Pat Riley

He had a presence. People listened to him. He looked like he belonged up there.

Mark Heisler
on Pat Riley,
at the news conference
announcing Riley as head coach
of the Lakers, in 1982

For years, no one had taken him seriously. Everyone liked him but no one noticed the presence or sensed the potential. It was an object lesson in the requisites of charisma: Without an opportunity, Riley was anonymous; given a position of power, he began to radiate. He would make many more strides but none larger than this quantum leap from anonymity.

Mark Heisler
on Pat Riley's jump from the Lakers' broadcast booth to assistant coach to head coach

It was hard for him to crack the whip in the beginning like he did later on, because you don't't' want to rub anybody the wrong way.

Jerry Buss
owner (1979–),
on Pat Riley

He took charge but was careful at the same time. With us, you had to come in and be assertive. You had to take charge because you're talking about a lot of veterans at that time who were looking at him, like, "OK, are we gonna run over him? Or is he going to be the man?" You've got Kareem, Jamaal Wilkes, all those players.

Jerry Buss

on Pat Riley taking over the reins of the Lakers in 1982

I felt that one thing he really did that many coaches weren't able to do: Pat didn't try to overcoach the team during games.

David Wohl

three-year Lakers assistant coach under Pat Riley

You gotta get totally out of yourself and into the unity of the team. The spirit of unity does not guarantee you anything, but without it you can't be successful.

Pat Riley

Pat Riley is an excellent Xs and Os coach. He wants you to carry out everything exactly the way he's drawn it on the blackboard, whether it's in practice or in a game. He wants you to carry out his instructions, whether it's how to play defense against a particular player or how to execute a certain strategy he believes might be the key to the game.

Magic Johnson

Everything was done for the good of the team. Pat drove that home. That was the philosophy. He didn't care if you had to stay up all night to do your part.

Gary Vitti
Lakers trainer (1985–), on Riley

He knows how to put a team together. That's always been his biggest asset. He makes the nucleus jell. He takes the players' strengths and potential and tries to bring it all together and make it work for everybody.

A. C. Green
on Pat Riley

If you go back in history to the Crusades, he would be like King Richard. The job focuses his attention almost completely. He'll have a few words to say if he runs into you. He's always cordial. He's always polite. But he's kind of a man on a mission.

David Wohl
on Pat Riley

Pat totally engulfed himself in this thing. Other guys are into music or cars. Pat was like, when he left here, instead of listening to music, he put in a motivational tape to get ready for the next practice.

Gary Vitti

Pat Riley is the reason we became a family. We had talent and wanted to win, but little things would creep in to divide us. He came in and changed us. He said, "Look, we got to take care of each other and not let things outside the family upset the family." From now on, nobody goes in the papers and talks about each other. You come in here and we straighten it out.

Magic Johnson

The players don't like to have a leash around their neck all the time. You have to trust the players. You have to allow them to be able to create and to become spontaneous.

Pat Riley

We didn't see eye to eye on a lot of issues, but I respected him because of what he had done. He gave all of the players respect. Now that I look back on it, I even respect him more because of what he helped us achieve. He's probably the best coach in the game.

Byron Scott
guard/forward (1984–93, 1997), on Pat Riley

Fast Fact: Riley guided the Lakers to four championships and seven total finals appearances during his nine-year tenure as Lakers court boss.

Pat Riley's contribution was difficult to gauge from a distance, but in person, you knew. He was an intense competitor. Our practices were like our games.

Jerry West

The thing that allowed Pat to be the way he was, he had the backing from above. Jerry West backed him. They would have a lot of disagreements but they were good friends. They arrived at things from a different approach, but they were in basic agreement on what the team needed to do to win.

David Wohl
on Riley

There is a difference between winning a championship and being a championship team.

Pat Riley

I think they're gonna be happy with Phil. He's gonna give them a certain structure and a certain guidance that they probably need. They got the talent. It's always been there. It's just how you utilize the talent in a focused situation. And I think Phil is good at that.

Michael Jordan

Chicago Bulls guard/forward and five-time NBA MVP, on the coming of Phil Jackson to Los Angeles

Phil Jackson seemed the perfect Laker choice not because he added more pressure, but because he seemed to lessen it for everybody else.

Los Angeles Times

on Phil Jackson's hiring prior to the 1999–2000 season

I believe the majority of coaching is done before the game.

Phil Jackson

Phil understands the game better than most people. And he expects certain things that he knows his guys can give him. He knows when to push his players, when not to push 'em. He knows who to yell at, who not to yell at. He knows who can take it. And he treats you like a man, as opposed to downplaying you or talking to you like you're less than him because of his position. He's a great coach. He laughs and smiles at life.

John Salley
on Jackson

He allowed you to have input. I liked that about him. With some coaches, it's like, "I'm the coach. I'm the man with the power."

Brian Shaw
on Phil Jackson

It was funny to see him and hear him walking through the locker room chanting and beating on his drum. Sometimes he was smiling, sometimes he was chanting. Sometimes he was just hitting it.

Derek Fisher

on coach Phil Jackson's unorthodox incorporations of Zen Buddhism and Native American customs into his coaching philosophy

You are successful only at the moment that you perform the successful act.

Tex Winter

Phil Jackson viewed coaching as a kind of parenting, with the parental goal of guiding its subjects toward independence. . . . It was important for the players to develop the faith in themselves that comes from making your own decisions.

Elizabeth Kaye

The way he handles the players, his motivation, his personal relationship with the players, I think this is his strength. That's borne out by the fact that they'll accept his coaching, they'll accept the criticism, even though sometimes it's pretty severe with certain players. They accept that because it's who he is, because he's Phil.

Tex Winter

on Jackson

He's the white version of my father. I do something spectacular, he sits there and goes, "So what?" He doesn't let me lose my focus. He stays on me all the time. That's what I like. It's what I need.

Shaquille O'Neal

on Phil Jackson

He wants a tenth title, which would make him the winningest coach in NBA history. That would be more titles than Red Auerbach won with the Boston Celtics. That would be his reason for coming back.

Tex Winter
on Phil Jackson's return to the Lakers prior to the 2005–06 season

Once you win, the goal to repeat may not be as strong as the original goal to win.

Phil Jackson

Don't let your successes go to your head or let your failures go to your heart.

Note posted in Phil Jackson's house

Teamwork is a nebulous thing. It is as ephemeral as love, disappearing at the latest insult.

Phil Jackson

When you have a system of offense, you can't be a person that just is taking the basketball trying to score. You have to move the basketball, because . . . you have to share the basketball with everybody. When you do that, you're sharing the game, and that makes a big difference.

Phil Jackson

If I don't try to squeeze the most out of my players, what good am I? Better yet, what good are they?

Phil Jackson

Players must be willing to take direction. Like they say in the military, in the time it takes to question an order, you might be dead.

Phil Jackson

Fouling out certainly wasn't what Dr. James Naismith had in mind when he invented the game in the 1890s. According to one of the original 13 rules Naismith devised, the player responsible for committing the second infraction left the court until the opposing squad scored a goal.

Phil Jackson

The most useful advice I ever received about coaching came from Al McGuire, the late Marquette leader and TV analyst. He said, "If it can't be done in eight hours, it can't be done."

Phil Jackson

The best players in the world are not immune to insecurity.

Phil Jackson

I prefer to see players develop a warrior mentality, in which they honor their opponent. . . . Your opponent is who makes you a better warrior.

Phil Jackson

Unless there is a complete breakdown, which is rare in playoff basketball, every game will be winnable in the last five or six minutes.

Phil Jackson

Free throws are the easiest shots in the game. There is no defender in your face, no contact.

Phil Jackson

Phil Jackson was a mystic masquerading as a coach, or the other way around.

Mark Heisler

SHRINE TO NO. 99

George Mikan is the greatest all-around basketball player who ever lived and the greatest gate attraction. He's the Ruth, the Dempsey, the Hagan, the Tilden of basketball.

Joe Lapchick

Anybody who doesn't know who George Mikan is, is not a basketball fan.

Kevin Garnett
nine-time Minnesota Timberwolves all-star forward

Six-foot–10 with thick glasses, Mikan was so effective as a center at DePaul that he forced the NCAA to adopt the goaltending rule.

Associated Press

When you start people thinking about changing the rules, you are a pretty good player. George was a guy that initiated the thinking about widening the lane. Early on, the lane was six feet wide. You could not have a guy as good as he was that close to the hoop. Through my time as a player, if you had taken George Mikan and put him on any team in the league, they were a potential championship team.

Earl Lloyd

Hall of Fame forward for three NBA teams (1951, 1953–60)

When it came to winning, Big George could be very tough and just a little mean. Toward the end of a ball game, if we were ahead by 20, George would come over to the bench and say, "Let's beat 'em good. Let's kick the hell out of 'em so they don't want to play us ever again."

Jim Pollard

Once he stationed himself under the basket, he was tough to push out. For rival players it must've been like trying to move the Statue of Liberty.

Jim Pollard
on George Mikan

He wanted to be number one, wanted you to be a little fearful of him on the court.

Jim Pollard
on Mikan

If you let Mikan get position, it was over. He would back in to the basket and go to work with those elbows.

Mike Bloom
two-year NBA forward (1948, '49) with Boston, Chicago

Mikan was great with those elbows. He used to kill our centers. Used to knock 'em down, draw the foul. Then help 'em up and pat 'em on the fanny.

Paul Seymour

His elbows should be in the Hall of Fame.

Ed Macauley
seven-time NBA all-star center/ forward,
who once lost a tooth defending Mikan

One night the marquee outside Madison Square Garden read: "Tonite: Geo. Mikan vs. the Knicks." More than anything, that incident summed up George Mikan's stature in those early years of the game. He was the league's draw.

Vern Mikkelsen

From time to time, there'd be problems between Pollard and Mikan. They were both great athletes, but George did most of our scoring and got most of the recognition. Our offense was built around George, and it would have been stupid not to use him.

Vern Mikkelsen

AP / Wide World Photo

George Mikan

He was a hell of a competitor. We'd get through a game and his question was, "Did we win?" That made us all on George's side, because he was a winner. George and I always argued, but when we stepped on the floor, we always played to win, the hell with who got the points.

Jim Pollard

George Mikan had a tremendous total confidence that he could get the job done. He would make believers out of us. Late in close games he always wanted the ball. The tremendous competitor that he was, he would say, "Let me have the ball. I'll get it done." More often than not, he did.

Vern Mikkelsen

It was Ray Meyer who transformed George Mikan from the lumbering giant who drew Frankenstein jokes into a pivot Hercules. It came slowly, the transformation, beginning with Meyer insisting that Mikan learn nimble footwork by always dancing with the smallest girls.

John Christgau

Mikan ran the whole show. He was an athlete despite what some people say about his bulk, and nobody ever had better offensive moves under the basket. When George played, he owned that lane.

Larry Foust

twelve-year NBA center/forward who played with the Lakers from 1958 through 1960

Mikan was an unlikely matinee idol. He had wavy hair, Coke-bottle glasses, and a gentle demeanor, having studied for the priesthood. He weighed 265 pounds and, if not a graceful student, could hook with either hand and had a soft touch. His career free-throw percentage was 77 percent, which would be impressive for a big man now. This was no dinosaur. Mikan was the first giant NBA center to walk erect.

Mark Heisler

He was a godsend to the NBA. He literally transcended the sport. In the '40s and '50s, the league was at the bottom of the totem pole. Whatever attention we were getting, pretty much was thanks to George.

Bob Cousy

Boston Celtics Hall of Fame guard

Nobody gave George Mikan anything. He earned his baskets.

Jim Pollard

He jump-started the NBA.

Dolph Schayes

Hall of Famer and one of the NBA's 50 Greatest Players, on Mikan

George Mikan is the greatest competitor I've ever seen in sports.

Bud Grant

forward (1950–51), later Hall of Fame football coach of the Minnesota Vikings

FAST FACT: By 1954, his last full season in the NBA, the colossal Lakers center had sustained two broken legs, broken bones in both feet, fractures of the wrist, nose, thumb and three fingers, and received 166 stitches from playing both college and pro basketball.

George Mikan is six-foot-ten. He couldn't have been greater if he was ten-foot-six.

Oscar Fraley

United Press International sportswriter (1940–65)/author of The Untouchables *with Eliot Ness*

MAJOR MOMENTS

That was something to behold. It was another level. I've seen some remarkable games, but I've never seen one like that before.

Phil Jackson
on Kobe Bryant's astronomical 81-point performance in a 122–104 Lakers win over the Toronto Raptors, January 22, 2006, the second highest single-game point total in NBA history

Jim Pollard leaps almost straight up. Off the wrong foot! Executed by anyone else the shot would be a disaster. But from Pollard, who some say is the smoothest, most graceful player ever in the game, the shot is a floating ballet move during which his arms and legs all seem to be moving together effortlessly despite the wrong-foot vertical launch. . . . The ball slips over the front rim. The huge crowd expresses its wonder by oooooooooo-ing, as if they have had the wind knocked out of them.

John Christgau
on the third basket of the legendary first contest between the Minneapolis Lakers and the Harlem Globetrotters, February 19, 1948, at Chicago Stadium, before a standing-room-only crowd of 17,823

I tried to beat the Globetrotters all by myself.

George Mikan
blaming himself for the Lakers' "Duel of the Century" loss to the Harlem Globetrotters in the two teams' initial encounter in February 1948. Mikan played well in his personal matchup with fabled Trotters center and clown nonpareil Goose Tatum, but the Globetrotters prevailed, 61–59, on a 30-foot buzzer-beater by Ermer Robinson

On January 20, 1952, George Mikan had his best game ever as he scored 61 points in a double-overtime win over Rochester. With 22 field goals and 17 free throws, Mikan came within two points of Joe Fulks's NBA record.

Stew Thornley

In what the Minneapolis Lakers viewed as their sweetest championship, they blasted the New York Knicks three straight in New York's old 69th Regiment Armory.

Roland Lazenby

on the Lakers' title run in 1953, in which Minneapolis abruptly lost homecourt advantage to the Knicks, losing the opening game at Minnesota. The Lakers eked out a two-point win in Game 2, before heading to New York, where they surprisingly swept the Knicks three straight

Sharman has Wilt playing like Russell.

Joe Mullaney

head coach (1970–71),
after the elevation of Chamberlain to team captain
during the 1971–72 championship season

The Lakers went off on what both Bill Sharman and Jack Ramsay called the finest stretch of basketball they'd ever seen. Within three minutes, the Lakers outscored the 76ers, 18–1, and ran away with the game.

Charley Rosen

on L.A.'s 25th straight win during its historic 33-game winning streak in the 1971–72 season, a 154–132 victory over Philadelphia. The game had been tied three times, and the Sixers led by one, with seven minutes remaining, before the blowout began

It's tougher to have a streak like this in basketball. We're in town for one night and then it's on to the next game. Baseball teams stay two or three days in one city before moving on.

Bill Sharman

on the Lakers' 33-game winning streak

The Lakers' total dominance of the NBA in November and December of 1971, and in the early days of January 1972, remains an extraordinary achievement that is not likely to be surpassed in any American professional sport.

Charley Rosen

on the Lakers' 33-game winning streak, the NBA equivalent of Joe DiMaggio's 56-game hitting streak in baseball or Johnny Unitas's 47-game streak with at least one TD pass in pro football

Wilt should be the MVP in the league this season.

Elgin Baylor

on the Big Dipper's outstanding both-ends play during L.A.'s legendary 33-game win streak during the 1971–72 season, to this day the longest win streak in the history of professional team sports

The patient is critical and about to die.

Walt "Clyde" Frazier

New York Knicks Hall of Fame guard, following the Knicks' demoralizing 116–111 overtime loss to L.A. in Game 4 of the 1972 NBA Finals, in which Lakers forward Jim McMillian's three straight jumpers in OT snuffed out any New York hope of victory. Los Angeles went on to win the title in five games, its first league crown since the George Mikan era (1954)

It's an unbelievable feeling, something I've always wanted to experience. Now I know what it feels like to be a champion.

Jerry West

tasting the fruits of NBA Finals success in 1972 after seven previous championship-round failings

The blow sounded like a melon striking concrete.

John Radcliffe

on the horrific blow from the fist of Lakers forward Kermit Washington that shattered the face of the Houston Rockets' Rudy Tomjanovich in December 1977. Washington was suspended by the league for 60 days and fined; Tomjanovich returned the following season but never achieved his former level of all-star play. Washington was dealt to the Celtics not long after the incident

No one will ever forget Magic's opening night in the pros when he leaped into the arms of Kareem Abdul-Jabbar after he hit a skyhook to beat the L.A. Clippers on national television.

Jerry West

at the conclusion of Magic Johnson's NBA (1979–80) debut

In the spring of 1980, a wide-eyed 20-year-old-still-wet-behind-the-ears-would-be-college-junior point guard stepped toward center court inside the Spectrum in Philadelphia at the onset of Game 6 of the NBA Finals and proceeded to create an unfathomable work of art.

Roy S. Johnson

author,
on Johnson's climax to his phenomenal freshman season in the NBA, closing out the championship finals with a 42-point, 15-rebound, seven-assist performance, during which the versatile Johnson played every position on the floor, including center, in the absence of ailing Lakers pivot Kareem Abdul-Jabbar

I felt like I could do anything.

Magic Johnson

on his memorable Game 6 performance to close out the 1980 championship series against the Philadelphia 76ers

On the first play, he came down in the low post and took a turnaround hook shot. He took a Kareem hook shot. The rest of the game, he played everywhere. He played guard. He played forward. Everyone sees him as playing center. That helped us. People forget Jamaal Wilkes had 37 points in that game.

Paul Westhead

on Magic Johnson's performance for the ages in the Lakers' Game 6 triumph over Philadelphia to take the 1980 NBA crown, four games to two. In that game, Johnson handled the center jump then played all four of the remaining floor positions during the 123–107 victory

I had to adjust to coming off the bench for the first time in my life. I was used to playing 40 to 45 minutes a game. In L.A., I was playing 15 minutes a game, and that was hard to deal with. Then we got to the playoffs and everything changed. I went from 15 minutes up to 30 to 40 minutes. It was crunch time, what I call pit bull time. You put your best out on the floor. We had a playoff run that was just unbelievable.

Robert McAdoo

forward/center (1982–85), on the 1981–82 Lakers 21–3 late-season run en route to the NBA championship. L.A. went 12–2 in the playoffs, at one point sweeping nine consecutive games

Fast Fact: The Lakers signed McAdoo—a former league MVP, two-time scoring champion, and future Hall of Famer—as a free agent prior to the start of the season.

Well, it's only one of about 90 I held.

Wilt Chamberlain

when asked about Kareem Abdul-Jabbar breaking Chamberlain's NBA career scoring record of 31,419 points in 1984

It was a loss that should never have happened. It was probably the worst loss in Lakers franchise history. We should have won in four straight games. It just made me crazy. It was just unforgivable. But I've been through all that before and I know what that's like, to lose when you don't want to lose.

Jerry West

on the Lakers' heartbreaking seven-game series loss to Boston in the 1984 NBA Finals, leaving L.A. 0–7 all time against the Celtics in the championship round

In the spring of 1984, when Kareem Abdul-Jabbar was closing in on the all-time scoring record, I made it clear that I wanted to make the pass that led to the record-breaking point. I told everybody: That assist is mine! . . . I floated a soft one-handed pass over Utah Jazz defender Rickey Green's head. Kareem caught the ball, faked a couple of times, then spun around for his patented sky-hook from about 15 feet out. It was dead on target, and the place went wild. It was a great moment, one I'm glad I can tell my kids I was a part of.

Magic Johnson

on the April 5, 1984, NBA milestone

That game was the turning point in Lakers history, I think. We came back strong and Kareem led the way. Riley, too. He stepped forward. It was the turning point in his career, too. He took his coaching to another level.

James Worthy
on Game 1 of the 1985 NBA Finals, the infamous Memorial Day Massacre, in which the Lakers were blown out at Boston, 148–114. The loss was especially galling, coming off the Celtics' mocking, in-your-face, comeback triumph over L.A. in the '84 finals. The Lakers regrouped, however, storming back behind Kareem Abdul-Jabbar's MVP performance to finally nail Boston, four games to two

The Garden was nearly empty. One of my old friends and I slipped out to the center of the Garden parquet. We giggled and exchanged high fives. The most odious sentence in all of sport—the Lakers have never beaten the Celtics—wasn't true anymore.

Jerry Buss
following L.A.'s 4–2 triumph over Boston in the 1985 NBA Finals, finally avenging the Celtics' stranglehold on the Lakers, who had lost seven previous times to Boston in the championship round

When I think about my biggest shot, there's no doubt that it came in Game 4 of the 1987 finals against Boston. We were leading, two games to one, but the Celtics were up by one point with less than 10 seconds left. I started to drive. Kevin McHale was right with me, and Robert Parrish jumped out to help. Suddenly my mind went clear: the sky-hook. It was one of those situations that went in slow motion. When the ball went through the net, all you could hear was about fifteen guys screaming their heads off. Other than that, it was silent inside Boston Garden, which is one of the best sounds I'll ever hear.

Magic Johnson

If you knew Isiah, if you knew Magic, the kiss was no big deal. They were going through some tough times because they were both trying to dance with the same girl. And there was only one partner.

Joe Dumars

Detroit Pistons Hall of Fame guard,

on the celebrated peck and hand-holding between the two longtime friends and court foes prior to Game 1 of the 1988 NBA Finals

We had 'em on the ropes, but we couldn't get 'em down.

Adrian Dantley

Detroit Pistons and onetime Lakers forward (1978–79), on Game 6 of the 1988 NBA Finals, in which Detroit—just 60 seconds away from defeating the Lakers for its first-ever league crown—couldn't hold a three-point lead, losing to L.A., 103–102, behind two Kareem Abdul-Jabbar free throws. Two nights later the Lakers swiped Game 7 for their fifth and final crown of the 1980s

I will cherish this the rest of my life, no matter what happens. I'm in a dream right now, and I don't ever want to wake up.

Magic Johnson

after being named MVP of the NBA's 42nd All-Star Game, in 1992—an honor he had predicted before the contest—with 25 points and nine assists. In the game's final minutes, Johnson successfully defended Isiah Thomas one on one, nailed a three-pointer, shut down Michael Jordan one on one, then closed with another trey. Prior to the season, Johnson had announced his retirement from the NBA because of testing positive for HIV

To knock down the shots that he knocked down in that game, it was only something that great players have the ability to do. At such a young age he put a notch on his belt for taking his place as one of the greatest players to ever play the game.

Derek Fisher

on Kobe Bryant's Game 4 performance in overtime during the 2000 NBA Finals against Indiana. With Shaquille O'Neal having fouled out, coach Phil Jackson spread the floor, allowing Bryant's unique one-on-one skills to produce eight of his 28 total points, including a game-winning reverse tip that carried the Lakers to a 120–118 victory and a 3–1 lead in the series

Phil beat his drum with a persistence on the morning of our last game. Everybody on the team seemed to perk up at the sound of it. We heard it. It made a difference.

Brian Shaw

on Jackson's percussive display prior to Game 6 of the 2000 NBA Finals against Indiana. That night the Lakers, behind Finals MVP Shaquille O'Neal's 41 points, dropped the Pacers, 116–111, for their first championship since 1988

I suppose I should marvel at the two shots he made. I don't. I've seen too much from him, from Michael. I am gratified.

Phil Jackson

following Kobe Bryant's two three-pointers—one to tie the game, the other to win it in double overtime—in the 2004 season-finale 105–104 victory at Portland, to give the Lakers the Pacific Division crown

Derek really believes in himself. He wants to hit a last-second shot.

Phil Jackson

to his assistant coaches sometime prior to Fisher's Game 5 buzzer-beater that downed San Antonio, 74–73, giving L.A. a 3–2 lead in the 2004 Western Conference semifinals

Bill Bertka had a phrase for whenever an unheralded player rose to the occasion. He called it paying the rent. In the fourth quarter of the biggest game of his life, Kareem Rush paid the rent.

Phil Jackson

on the reserve guard's trio of fourth-quarter lights-out three-pointers that lifted L.A. to a 96–90 Game 6 win over Minnesota in the 2004 Western Conference finals, putting the Lakers into their fourth NBA Finals appearance in five seasons

By halftime, he had 26 points—not a bad tally for most players. By the end of the game, he had put up the second-highest total in NBA history. The Los Angeles Lakers star scored a staggering 81 points Sunday night against the Toronto Raptors in a 122–104 win. Only Wilt Chamberlain's 100-point game stands ahead of him.

Associated Press

January 22, 2006,
on Kobe Bryant's milestone scoring achievement

It just happened, man. To sit here and say I grasp what happened, that would be lying. Not even in my dreams.

Kobe Bryant

after scoring 81 points against Toronto, on January 22, 2006, breaking Elgin Baylor's club mark of 71, set in 1960

I never imagined I would see history like that. I can't tell you where that came from. He just kept attacking, attacking, attacking—every time he got the ball.

Devean George
on teammate Kobe Bryant's performance for the ages, January 22, 2006

You're sitting and watching, and it's like a miracle unfolding in front of your eyes and you can't accept it. Somehow, the brain won't work.

Jerry Buss
on watching Kobe's 81-point fusillade in a win against the Raptors

To put Kobe's superhuman Sunday into some perspective, NBA teams have been held below 81 points 88 times this season.

Chris Ramsay
ESPN.com, January 22, 2006

Kobe Bryant calmly rose to another historic performance of the NBA's best one-man show. Bryant became the youngest player to score 16,000 points, finishing with 42 in the Lakers' 106–94 victory over Golden State.

Greg Beacham

Associated Press sportswriter, March 4, 2006

He started when he was 17. It's great, but it's not the stuff I care about. It's something he'll look back on some day and say, "That's remarkable."

Phil Jackson

on Bryant's ascent to the 16,000-point mark

If he picks up the paper and reads about it, he should know that I owe a lot of it to him and to the other great players as well, because I really learned a lot about the game from watching them. I just steal all of their moves and incorporate them into my game. I copied Elgin's first step. It's actually a "rocker" step, which is kind of a stutter move.

Kobe Bryant

whose 50 points in a 110–99 victory over the Portland Trail Blazers, on April 14, 2006, broke Elgin Baylor's single-season Lakers scoring record

It was the most fun shot I've ever hit.

Kobe Bryant

on his looping baseline runner with seven-tenths of a second left in the fourth quarter to force overtime and a 17-footer as time expired to lift the Lakers to an improbable 99–98 victory over the Phoenix Suns and a 3–1 lead in the 2006 first-round Western Conference playoff series

THE LAKERS ALL-TIME TEAM

Nothing in all of Lakerdom generates more excitement than the great players who have worn the Purple & Gold. Picking an all-time team from this esteemed franchise that dates back to the 1947–48 season in Minneapolis is a Herculean undertaking.

While no-brainers exist in the selection of forward Elgin Baylor and guards Jerry West and Magic Johnson, imagine leaving Kobe Bryant, two Hall of Fame centers and one future HOF center sitting on the pine! Modern-day followers might put James Worthy or Jamaal Wilkes at a forward spot, but they aren't aware of the mercurial "Kangaroo Kid," Jim Pollard, the original prototype of the Jordanesque leaper and a tenacious defender who seldom fouled.

To contemplate, cajole, stroke and extol: herein for your argumentative pleasure is the Lakers All-Time Team.

Jim Pollard

Forward (1948–55)

All-BAA first team (1949), All-NBA first team (1950), All-NBA second team (1952, '54), Basketball Hall of Fame (1978), Lakers head coach (1960)

We used to know when Pollard had been in the building, because the tops of the backboards would be clean where he raked them. Pollard was fast, too. You couldn't press him either. He was too good moving with the ball. He'd get by you in a cat lick.

Horace "Bones" McKinney

six-year BAA-NBA player (1947–52)/ Wake Forest head coach (1958–65)/ Carolina Cougars (ABA) head coach (1969–71)

In 1950 the Associated Press voted George Mikan the Greatest Basketball Player of the Half Century, but two years later, another poll was taken among players who had been in the league since its inception. Their pick as the greatest player ever? Jim Pollard.

Stew Thornley

Elgin Baylor

Forward (1959–72)

Nine-time NBA All-Star Game selection,
NBA All-Star Game co-MVP (1959),
NBA Rookie of the Year (1959),
10-time All-NBA first team selection

He had that wonderful, magical instinct for making plays and doing things that you had to just stop and watch. I hear people talking about forwards today. I don't see many that can compare to him.

Jerry West
on Elgin Baylor

He's the greatest find since Jim Pollard.

John Kundla
on Baylor

He just might be the best player I ever saw. He was doing things that Dr. J. made famous 20 years later.

Chick Hearn
on Baylor

Kareem Abdul-Jabbar

Center (1976–89)

NBA MVP (1976, '77, '80),
NBA Finals MVP (1985),
13-time NBA All-Star Game selection,
six-time All-NBA first team selection

I lived to play against Kareem Abdul-Jabbar. He was the greatest player I ever played against by far. Not even close. Better than Jordan. Better than Magic. Better than Bird. Better than Dr. J. Better than the best of the best that I played against. Better than Rick Barry. Nobody who ever played against Kareem Abdul-Jabbar will ever forget it. He was my source of motivation for everything I ever did. All the physical rehab from 32 operations, all the weight training, all the conditioning drills. Every day in practice it was always Jabbar, Jabbar, Jabbar.

Bill Walton

ten-year Hall of Fame center for Portland, San Diego-L.A. Clippers, and Boston/renowned TV analyst

Jerry West

Shooting Guard (1961–74),

NBA Finals MVP (1969),
14-time NBA All-Star Game selection,
NBA All-Star Game MVP (1972),
10-time All-NBA first team selection,
Lakers head coach (1977–79)

Jerry led the league in assists and still averaged 25 points a game and played great defense. Jerry West is probably the greatest defensive guard who ever played. People know him for scoring points, but he was so good on defense. Had quick hands and stole the ball. He stole more than anybody, although they didn't keep records on it then. And he'd come around behind shooters and block their shots from behind.

Bill Sharman

It was obvious from that first year (1961) that Jerry West was a superstar. He had tremendous speed and quickness and explosiveness.

Bob Cousy
Hall of Fame guard,
Boston Celtics

EARVIN "MAGIC" JOHNSON

Point Guard (1980–91, 1996)

NBA MVP (1987, '89, '90),
NBA Finals MVP (1980, '82, '87),
12-time NBA All-Star Game selection,
NBA All-Star Game MVP (1990, '92),
nine-time All-NBA first team selection,
J. Walter Kennedy Citizenship Trophy (1992),
Lakers head coach (1994)

I thought I'd seen it all when it came to basketball—every style, every size and shape player there was. . . . I'd seen shorter-than-average centers, taller-than-average guards, and players with more talent than you might have thought was possible. I'd played against and been teammates with guys like Oscar Robertson, Bill Russell, and Wilt Chamberlain, three of the best players who ever lived. And then I saw Magic Johnson.

Jerry West

Pat Riley

Coach (1982–90)

Four NBA championships (1982, '85, '87, '88), NBA Coach of the Year (1990), winningest coach in Lakers history (635–241 overall, including postseason)

As much as Pat Riley demands discipline, he's also a player's coach. He understands the players' hearts and minds. He knows when to push us and when to back off. Pat knows how to sense problems and bring them out into the open before they tear us apart. . . . He's also aggressive, and that's how we play. He's intense, and that's also how we play.

Magic Johnson

I think the one thing I did accomplish with this team is to maintain its excellence. We didn't break it down, and screw it up, and overcoach it. We maintained.

Pat Riley
on his 1980s Lakers dynasty

Lakers All-Time Team

First Team

Jim Pollard (1948–55), *forward*

Elgin Baylor (1959–72), *forward*

Kareem Abdul-Jabbar (1976–89), *center*

Jerry West (1961–74), *shooting guard*

Earvin "Magic" Johnson (1980–91, 1996), *point guard*

Pat Riley (1982–90), *coach*

Second Team

James Worthy (1983–94), *forward*

Vern Mikkelsen (1950–59), *forward*

George Mikan (1947–54, 1956), *center*

Kobe Bryant (1997–), *guard*

Gail Goodrich (1966–68, 1971–76), *guard*

John Kundla (1948–57, 1958–59), *coach*

THE GREAT LAKERS FIVES

On the Lakers, we believe we're all stars, from the starters to the last man on the bench. Everybody plays a role in the team's success. When they hand out championship rings, they don't just give them to the MVP. Everybody gets one. Twelve guys, twelve rings. The team.

Magic Johnson

The Lakers were a great team. George Mikan and Vern Mikkelsen and Jim Pollard and Slater Martin—they could have played today. Mikkelsen would be making $2 million a year, for God sakes. These people today don't realize how good they were.

Marty Blake

former Hawks GM/longtime scout, on the Minneapolis dynasty of the late 1940s-mid '50s

The 1953–54 Laker team included four players who would eventually be inducted into the Basketball Hall of Fame: George Mikan, Jim Pollard, Slater Martin, and newcomer Clyde Lovellette, who was being groomed as Mikan's successor.

Stew Thornley

They were the Celtics West. Everybody except Wilt just tore ass downcourt as fast as they could. . . . It was a four-man break with the wingmen switching sides along the baseline and popping back up to the ball. And when they couldn't run themselves into a good shot, there was always Wilt to go to in a half-court setup. That team could score quickly and from just about anywhere.

Tom Heinsohn
nine-year Boston Celtics forward/ Celtics head coach (1970–78), on the 1972 NBA champion Lakers

The day Elgin Baylor announced his retirement the Lakers began their 33-game win streak. The 1971–72 Lakers would win more games than any other team in NBA history—with a 69–13 record that wouldn't be bested for a quarter of a century.

Roland Lazenby

Wilt liked records, so during the streak he played the best defense of his career.

Nate Thurmond

fourteen-year NBA center with San Francisco-Golden State, Chicago, and Cleveland, on the likely never-to-be-duplicated 33-game win streak reeled off by the Lakers during the 1971–72 championship season

They'd been so invincible for so long. The streak was them, and they were the streak.

Charley Rosen

on the Lakers' record-breaking 33-game win streak in 1971–72

The Lakers have to be the greatest team in the history of the game. I thought so before the game and tonight confirmed it. We played a perfect game for about 45 minutes, and we still couldn't beat them. The capper is that the Lakers didn't even play nearly as well as they can.

Steve Patterson
Cleveland Cavaliers forward (1972–76),
after L.A.'s 32nd consecutive win in 1971–72, a 113–103 victory over the Cavs

We'll get another one going. We'll start Tuesday night in Detroit and call it Son of Streak.

Frank O'Neill
former Lakers trainer,
after the Lakers' 33-game win streak ended in a 120–104 loss at Milwaukee, January 9, 1972

This was a very intelligent group of players who always kept their poise and usually won the close games. They were able to adjust to every situation. . . . We won because the players were mature and dedicated.

Bill Sharman
on his world champion 1972 Lakers

I played terrible basketball in the finals and yet we won. That didn't seem fair for me personally because I had contributed so much in other years when we lost. Now, when we won, I was just another piece of the machinery. It was particularly frustrating because I was playing so poorly that the team had to overcome me. Maybe that's what a team is all about.

Jerry West
on the NBA champion '72 Lakers

The main differences between the Chamberlain-West and the Jabbar-Magic teams was that the latter were even quicker and more finesse-oriented than the former. (Phil Jackson's Lakers champs of 2000–2002 were driven by the incomparable power of Shaquille O'Neal.)

Charley Rosen

Because of the 1972 Lakers, Hollywood, the land of the nutburger and the drive-in mortuary, became, and still is, the capital of professional basketball. Whether they win, lose, or draw, the on- and off-court doings of the Hollywood Lakers continue to be the league's biggest news.

Charley Rosen

On that one team you probably had more diverse, strong personalities than you had on any championship team in the history of the game.

Bill Bertka

on the 1971–72 world champion Lakers, comprised of Gail Goodrich, Happy Hairston, Jim McMillian, Pat Riley, Keith Erickson, and Flynn Robinson, along with superstars Wilt Chamberlain, Jerry West, and for part of the season, Elgin Baylor

The Lakers were just about a perfect team. Speed, strength, versatility, intelligence, outstanding leadership—they had it all. I've always believed that my Chicago Bulls championship teams in the late '90s would have easily handled Bill Russell's Celtics and Magic Johnson's Showtime Lakers. But the 1971–72 Lakers would have given us a battle royal.

Phil Jackson

It was probably the ultimate job of communicating that any Lakers' team has ever managed, and it won us a championship.

Magic Johnson
on his most exciting road moment—the Lakers' big Game 6 (the final game of the 1985 NBA championship series) win at Boston Garden. The Lakers silenced the frenzied partisan crowd after taking the lead late. Johnson attributes the title win to L.A.'s ability to ignore the Garden noise level, so loud at times that the players couldn't hear each other out on the floor

Those years with McAdoo, that team was awfully close. We were all so tough-minded. We would go on the road and say, "Okay, how many games we got?" We'd see there was six. "We're gonna win six." And then we'd go out and win all six. . . . That was the respect we had for one another. That was the sign of a true championship team.

Magic Johnson
on the 1985 world champion Lakers

This is the best team I've ever played against.

Larry Bird
on the '87 Lakers

This is a super team, the best I've played on. It's fast; they can shoot, rebound, we've got inside people, everything. I've never played on a team that had everything before. We've always had to play around something, but this team has it all.

Magic Johnson
on L.A.'s 1987 world champs

We knew in our heads couldn't nobody keep up. It was amazing watching that team play, how quick we scored on people, the kinds of passes. The ball'd never hit the floor. Bam, bam, bam, layup! Magic tips one in, Kareem, McAdoo comes off the bench. Just the foot speed!

Norm Nixon
guard (1978–83),
on the 1982 Lakers

The 1989 Lakers team was the best I ever saw. They were 11–0 going into the Finals against Detroit. Magic was in his prime. Orlando Woolridge was playing great ball. They had Mychal Thompson playing great ball. Byron Scott had a great season. They were tremendous.

Doug Krikorian

The first one's a novelty and it feels real good. The first one will always be the best one. The second one, the adversity that we went through throughout the course of the year made that one special. We proved that we belonged. And this one, it's kind of making us step up as one of the great teams.

Kobe Bryant

on the Lakers championship trifecta of 2000, 2001, and 2002

The 2001 Lakers knew they were an even better team than they had been the year before. The defense was better because their starters were better. Rick Fox defended better than Glen Rice, Horace Grant was better than A. C. Green, Derek Fisher was better than Ron Harper.

Elizabeth Kaye

The final contest of the season would be, in a sense, a coronation rite for the once and future kings, the game that would leave the Lakers with a 15–1 record in the playoffs—the best postseason of any NBA team ever.

Elizabeth Kaye

on the 2001 Lakers, who took the league crown four games to one over Philadelphia

The 2000–02 Los Angeles Lakers joined the Minneapolis Lakers, Bill Russell's Celtics, and Phil Jackson's Chicago Bulls as the only teams to win three straight titles.

Roland Lazenby

I've been around some great teams and some great players, but this truly was one of the most courageous efforts I've ever seen.

Phil Jackson

on the 2004 Lakers' four-games-to-two triumph over the defending NBA champion San Antonio Spurs in the Western Conference semifinals, after being down 0–2

THE GREAT RIVALRIES

I had to educate my players who the Celtics were. One day in practice, I asked if anyone knew. Finally Kareem raised his hand. He said the Celtics were a warring race of Danes who invaded Ireland.

Pat Riley

Between 1949 and 1954, the Minneapolis Lakers won 267 games. The Rochester Royals won 266. Twice the Royals finished ahead of Minneapolis in the regular-season standings. But in head-to-head meetings, the Lakers usually won (Lakers 38–28 vs. Royals). This old rivalry would strangely find a new life in the 21st century. The Rochester Royals would move to Cincinnati, then to Kansas City and Omaha, before settling in as the Sacramento Kings. Like their counterparts decades earlier, the Kings would battle furiously against the Lakers only to lose the big ones.

Roland Lazenby

To me, our games with Rochester, that was the greatest basketball ever played. There was some science to it, some finesse to it.

Sid Hartman

Portland remained the Lakers' nemesis. The two teams were one of basketballs' feuding couples. They had met in the playoffs nine times. They knew each other's strengths and weaknesses, and they knew how to push each other's buttons. Few teams considered themselves better than the Lakers, but Portland did. And they *were* better when you went player for player, one to 12.

Elizabeth Kaye
2001

This is the worst thing I've ever had to deal with.

Scottie Pippen
seventeen-year guard/forward for Chicago, Houston, and Portland, after the Trail Blazers were swept three straight by the Lakers in the opening round of the 2001 playoffs

Whenever we play the Celtics, it seems like we're playing in the last game that'll be played in basketball history.

Magic Johnson

Whenever the Lakers play the Celtics, I always have one eye on Larry Bird and he always has one eye on me. That's our little game. Our personal rivalry within the Lakers-Celtics rivalry is something that will always mean a lot to me. Larry has always given me something else to strive for and exceed: excellence. When we've beaten a Larry Bird team, the Lakers know we've beaten the best.

Magic Johnson

The Lakers/Celtics—that might have been the rivalry that built the NBA. Russell/Chamberlain, Bird/Magic.

Rick Telander

Chicago Sun-Times *columnist*

The Lakers were always the noble opposition when I started going to see NBA games as an eighth grader in 1960. They couldn't beat the Celtics. I was a Celtics fan in those days. But the Lakers were always interesting to watch because of Jerry West and Elgin Baylor. They went from being the loyal opposition to being a dominant team during the Showtime period.

Kareem Abdul-Jabbar

If you go back to the original Lakers in Minnesota, they won five NBA championships and one in the old National Basketball League. That was a great team. That was a team like the Celtics. Then when the Lakers moved to Los Angeles, they were good, but they couldn't win for a long time because they were always playing the Celtics.

Dr. Jack Ramsay

The Celtics were beating them every year. It's hard to underestimate the damage done to the Lakers psyche by all those Celtics victories. The Celtics were incredibly good about rubbing it in. Everybody hated the Celtics.

Mark Heisler

They had Cous and Russ and Sharman and Heinsohn and Frank Ramsey and the Jones boys, K. C. and Sam. It developed into a good rivalry. Some of the games were very intense.

Chick Hearn
on the 1960s Celtics teams that took six NBA Finals from Los Angeles

The Lakers perhaps didn't realize it at the time, but the 1962 playoffs were just one of the early steps in their shared history with the Celtics. They faced a decade of torment from Bill Russell's blocked shots and Red Auerbach's lit cigars.

Roland Lazenby
on the "first of The Curse": L.A.'s initial NBA Finals loss to Boston, in seven games

We had a great team and they had two great, great players. That was the measure of why that rivalry went that way all the time. Those two guys, Baylor and West, they're still at the top of my all-time list, on the starting five. Elgin Baylor as forward beats out Bird, Julius Erving, and everybody else. West was what I call a freak.

Tom Heinsohn

Where Wilt Chamberlain struggled most of his career out of context, Bill Russell always seemed to have the right coach, the right teammates, and they got the right results.

Roland Lazenby

We all have our own particular feelings when we lose. There's no gratification. I was searching everything that I'd ever done in my life for the reason, looking for an answer why. Why can't we get a bounce of the ball? It almost controlled my life. It was a controlling factor in my play. When we played against Boston, I wanted to play my very best. I didn't want any friends on the other team.

Jerry West

who appeared in nine NBA Finals with the Lakers, losing eight of them, six to Boston

It was a challenge to play against Bill Russell and the Celtics. It was fun. It was disappointing to lose. But it was the ultimate challenge. They were a proud team, and they had reason to be.

Elgin Baylor

It got to the point where Jerry hated anything green. Jerry told me he couldn't even wear a green sportcoat or a green shirt for a lot of years. Green really rubbed him the wrong way.

Bill Sharman

FAST FACT: West suffered a peculiar indignity after being named 1969 NBA Finals MVP, following L.A.'s heartbreaking seven-game series loss to archrival Boston: the car he was given for the honor was green.

The first year I came to Boston, the Celtics and Lakers got into it. Both benches emptied. I remember that when they began breaking it up, K. C. Jones was at the bottom of the pile and had Michael Cooper in a headlock. That's the first time I had ever seen an NBA coach in a fight with one of the players. But that was the Celtics and Lakers.

Jerry Sichting
former Boston Celtic and ten-year NBA guard

The Lakers used to think of the Celtics as cheap-shot artists, and we found ourselves thinking about nothing but retaliation. It went back and forth between us for a lot of years because both teams were trying to establish themselves as the very best in the game. If they took one of our men out then we'd take out one of their men. It got very dangerous. Now the two teams just play hard, as hard as we can when we face each other.

Magic Johnson

There was a little resentment between us, but as the years went on, we began to develop more of a friendship. Now we know we have the best rivalry in sports. We also have the ultimate respect for each other, which means we can battle each other on the court and keep it clean.

Magic Johnson
on his rivalry/friendship with Larry Bird

Fast Fact: Both Johnson and Bird entered the NBA in 1979, though neither knew the other. The media generated reams of copy on both players, an offshoot from their NCAA title-match showdown the previous spring, and basically created a rivalry from the beginning.

Larry Bird and I have shared a lot of things in our careers, but what we've respected most in each other was that we both loved to pass the basketball. And we loved to win.

Magic Johnson

That first series that we gave them in 1984 really seasoned us. It gave us the mental tenacity that we didn't always exhibit.

Kareem Abdul-Jabbar

on the deflating seven-game NBA Finals loss to the Celtics, a demoralizing continuation of the club's 0–6 record in the championship series against Boston dating back to 1962

It's like the bully on the block who keeps taking your lunch money every day. Finally you get tired of it and you whack him.

David Wohl

on the Lakers' redemptive NBA Finals win over Boston in 1985, their first-ever championship triumph over the Celtics after seven title-series losses

The Lakers' failures against the Celtics became the standard for basketball futility, and the spell wasn't broken until 1985, when Pat Riley coached Los Angeles past Boston for the league championship.

Dr. Jack Ramsay

I feel like Johnny Podres did in 1955.

Kareem Abdul-Jabbar
when the Lakers finally defeated Boston in the NBA Finals, in 1985, after losing seven previous times to the Celtics in the championship round

FAST FACT: Podres was the pitching star and World Series MVP for Brooklyn in '55, when the Dodgers finally beat their longtime nemesis, the New York Yankees, after five prior losses to the Bronx Bombers in the World Series.

For everyone on the team it was probably one of the most painful trials an athlete could ever go through. In some respects, it was humiliating that they could beat us year after year like that. But realistically, except for two years, we shouldn't have beaten them. They were just better than us.

Jerry West

on the Lakers' 0–7 run against the Boston Celtics in NBA Finals play, before their breakthrough win in 1985

It left a lot of scars on me, a lot of scars.

Jerry West

on the overwhelming imbalance of the NBA Finals contested between the Boston Celtics and the L.A. Lakers during West's playing career, in which Boston took all six championship series

FANS

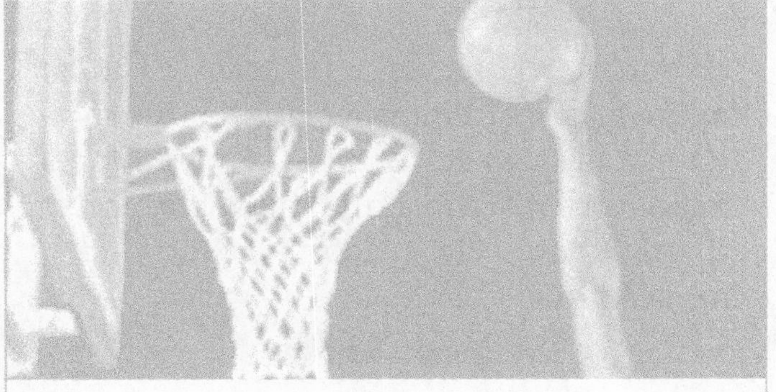

It was incredible. Going to watch the Lakers play became like going to watch a heavyweight fight 82 times a year. People dressed up. People were excited. People didn't know what was going to happen.

Jim Hill
longtime Los Angeles sportscaster, on the arrival of Magic Johnson and the Showtime Lakers of the early 1980s

Whenever Boston's in town, I start feelin' the excitement early that morning when I first wake up, then I turn on the radio and it's the only thing anybody's talking about. The Lakers and the Celtics are sold out.

Magic Johnson

Most nights everybody's laughin', talkin', and jokin' around, but when the Celtics are waiting for us, it's quiet.

Magic Johnson

Suddenly Hollywood embraced Lakers games as sort of a community lovefest. Everyone in town wanted to see the Magic parade.

Tex Winter

on the demand to see L.A.'s "Showtime" of the early eighties

The celebrities had tremendous impact. Put a guy like Jack Nicholson in the front row, and people will come to see the game and the star. . . . Doris Day and Pat Boone were big fans, on the sidelines all the time.

Chick Hearn

If we're in Boston, I just try to stay in my hotel room most of the day and shut out the distractions outside. There've been nights when someone has sneaked into the hotel and set off the fire alarm just so we'd lose sleep. After a while, we just expect it to happen.

Magic Johnson

Wilt was always the villain. Wherever Wilt went in those days he was always booed and unappreciated. But in tribute to the Lakers fans, from the day he stepped on the Forum floor, he was never booed, never shown disrespect. He was only appreciated.

Bill Bertka

The moment Magic smiled, I guess L.A. started smiling. The city before had not really gotten into the team, even though they had won that championship [in '72]. But these were younger guys, they were more outgoing, they were out around the town. They brought the town into the game.

Lou Adler
famous record producer

Certainly Jack Nicholson is an enthusiastic fan. He attends every home game unless he is shooting a film out of town, in which case the Lakers ship him videotapes of the games he missed.

Scott Ostler
Steve Springer

During the playoffs, Jack Nicholson frequently travels to Lakers road games. In Boston for the 1985 finals, he stirred up Celtic fans and was even accused of mooning the Boston Garden crowd. Although taped replays are inconclusive, the mooning has become part of the Laker-Celtic legend.

Scott Ostler
Steve Springer

13

THE BALL BAG

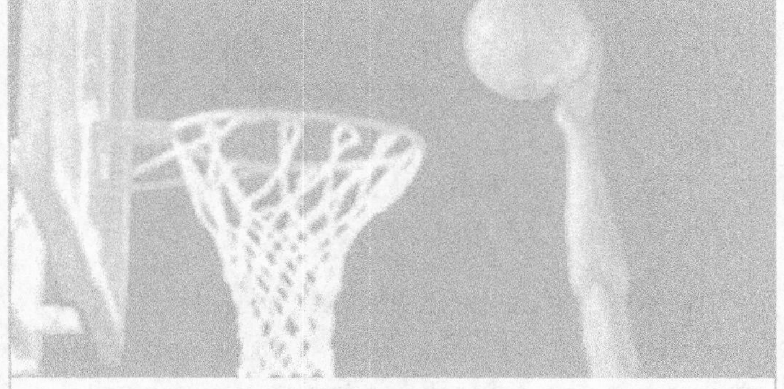

Here I am, the greatest scorer in the game of basketball, and I've been asked by many coaches not to score. Now, where else in a sport can you ask a guy to stop something he's the best in the world doing? It's like telling Babe Ruth not to hit home runs.

Wilt Chamberlain

Fast Fact: Two of Chamberlain's three coaches during his five seasons in Los Angeles asked the big man if he would sacrifice for the team and concentrate on rebounding and defense, not scoring.

I once told a friend that when Earvin Johnson, Jr., was born, he was sprinkled with Magic dust.

Jerry West

Earvin "Magic" Johnson wept the first time he donned a Lakers uniform in 1979.

Roland Lazenby

I'm always asked about which players I emulated when I was younger. Well, I tried to take a little bit from everybody—Dave Bing, Jerry West, Oscar Robertson, Wilt Chamberlain.

Magic Johnson

During my career, I've committed almost 2700 turnovers! Nearly 3000 mistakes! And I remember almost every one; they're my nightmares.

Magic Johnson
1989

It's been a tremendous lesson for Kobe that he can't control everything. Great players are used to imposing their will and controlling the things that allow them to succeed. All of a sudden, they come up against an out-of-control situation and realize there are things beyond their control. And that's a very maturing situation.

Phil Jackson

on Bryant's change in the aftermath of the 2003 Colorado rape charge and the Lakers' trail off as a team after the three successive championship seasons

I just want to be young, have fun, drink Pepsi, and wear Reebok.

Shaquille O'Neal

at the press conference announcing his $120 million signing with the Lakers in 1996

I think players, in general, used to be more well-rounded. Guys who were great scorers—Oscar Robertson, Rick Barry, Walt Frazier, and Pete Maravich—could also pass, rebound, and play defense with anybody.

Magic Johnson

He said the best skill I could have was a basketball mind.

Magic Johnson

on his dad's advice to Earvin Jr. as a youngster

A great pass is a thing of beauty. It's a Picasso or a Rembrandt.

Magic Johnson

Rebounding is probably the most passionate part of basketball. It's emotion; it's heart.

Magic Johnson

The lenses in George Mikan's glasses were a quarter-inch thick. He once said trying to see without them was like driving a car without wipers during a rainstorm.

Roland Lazenby

After we won, we had to hustle to catch a train out of Rochester. On the way out, we picked up a couple of six-packs. We put 'em in the stainless steel sink in the men's room on the train. Then we sat there and celebrated our first championship with the train rattling all around and the wheels rolling underneath.

Jim Pollard
on post-championship celebration, 1948-style

Fast Fact: The Lakers celebrated their first-ever pro basketball title in the 1947–48 season, claiming the National Basketball League crown after registering a 43–17 regular season mark, before disposing of Oshkosh, Tri-Cities, and Rochester in the playoffs.

You could see what made Jerry West great and what drove him. It was this nagging fear that he hadn't ever done anything. And then when he did do something, when they finally broke through in 1972 and won a title, he didn't know what to do. Pat Riley talks about how Jerry walked in and took a sip of champagne and just walked out. Didn't know what to do with victory.

Mark Heisler

There's married Lakers players who had a lot more sex than Wilt did. There was one who made Wilt look like an amateur.

Doug Krikorian

Magic put on performances you can't believe. Jordan was dominant in the '90s when ESPN and cable were big. People forget that cable wasn't that big in the '80s. Magic was phenomenal. Every game he played, he played great. He didn't give a damn about stats. He played in the NBA 12 seasons, and they were in the NBA Finals nine times. Does that tell you something about Magic?

Doug Krikorian

When our bus would pull up to a hotel, you'd see 60 people out there waiting and 40 of them would be women. It was like going around with a rock group.

Byron Scott

From Wilt Chamberlain's claim of making love to 20,000 women, to Magic Johnson's surprise announcement that he was HIV positive, to the prostitution solicitation charge against James Worthy, to the 2003 rape case against Kobe Bryant that garnered international attention, to Jeanie Buss, daughter of Lakers owner Jerry Buss, posing nude for *Playboy* in the team offices in 1994, the Lakers have made scandal a persistent part of their image.

Roland Lazenby

Shaq and I have never even talked about it. We communicate about it through the media mostly.

Kobe Bryant
on discussing their well-publicized difficulties in getting along, 1999

The guys broke down crying, the whole room. Everybody felt for Earvin. We felt like we had lost somebody, and yet he was still there.

Mike Dunleavy
head coach (1991–92), after Johnson's stunning address to teammates prior to the start of the 1991–92 season that he had tested HIV positive. Though he would play in 32 games in 1995–96, the condition effectively ended his outstanding 13-year NBA career

Then we all just went home and turned off our phones.

Gary Vitti
following Magic Johnson's press conference informing the world that he had tested HIV positive and was retiring from the Lakers

I'll never disappear. I don't know how to. I love to live. When you disappear, you stop living.

Magic Johnson

Phil Jackson was dealing with two mighty big egos. But in my mind, I blamed Shaq more than Kobe. Kobe tried to sacrifice. Kobe tried to please Shaq, because Kobe realized the team's effectiveness began with Shaq. But if you look at Shaq's quotes in the paper, it was always me, me, me. Give me the ball. It's my team, my city. Shaq is a wonderful person in a lot of ways. He's very compassionate, very generous. He has a great sense of humor. But he's moody; he's unpredictable. And he's very self-centered.

Tex Winter

You can't have two Batmans. You have to have one Batman and one Robin.

Horace Grant
forward (2001, 2004),
on having two superstars on the same team

I don't hate the guy. It's like being married. We need each other.

Shaquille O'Neal
on his turbulent relationship with Kobe Bryant when both were with the Lakers

Shaq wants to win as much as you do, and if you work well together, the two of you could be the greatest team in NBA history.

Jerry West
to Kobe Bryant during the 2001 season

A basic difference between Shaq and Kobe is that when you ask Shaq to do something, he'll say: "No, I don't want to do that." But after a little pouting, he will do it. Ask Kobe, and he'll say, "okay," and then he will do whatever he wants.

Phil Jackson

Shaq liked to quote philosophers. When he accepted the MVP trophy, he invoked Aristotle's observation that you are what you repeatedly do. That summer, as Shaq sightings occurred at what he called gentlemen's clubs and at Fatburger at three in the morning, that notion—you are what you repeatedly do—still had application.

Elizabeth Kaye

Unceasing change turns the wheel of life, and so reality is shown in all its many forms.

Phil Jackson mantra
for finding inner peace

Perhaps winning nine championships has helped me realize that the Larry O'Brien Trophy is not the key to finding real peace.

Phil Jackson

The first thing we would do when we got to a hotel was take out our uniforms and gear and hang it over the radiator so it would dry for the next game. You learned to live with that smell.

Vern Mikkelsen
on life on the road in the 1950s NBA

I decided to clean out Wilt Chamberlain's gym bag. Besides the dirty socks and jocks I also found several of Wilt's uncashed paychecks from the Lakers that were worth tens of thousands of dollars. All the checks smelled bad enough to be burned.

Frank O'Neill

He always wore a rubber band around his right wrist to remind him of the days when he was too poor to replace his sagging sweat socks and had to hold them up with elastic.

Bill Libby
on Wilt Chamberlain's wrist "jewelry"

At first, you go in and you try and get your numbers and do your thing. But later in your career, you realize that championships are more important. Wilt realized that later in his career, and I'm realizing it now in my career, too.

Shaquille O'Neal
during the 1999–2000 championship season, Shaq's eighth year in the league

14

LAKERS CHAMPIONSHIP ROSTERS

In the history of professional basketball, only one team has won more championships than the Lakers, their 15 titles placing second all time to Boston's 16. With six crowns logged in Minneapolis and nine in Los Angeles, many a Laker has played the cog in the wheel. The following roster listings are a salute to all the players that have helped raise championship banners for the Lakers.

1947–48

51–19

NBL champions
(includes 3–1 Western Division opening-round playoff win over Oshkosh, 2–0 Western Division semifinals win over Tri-Cities, and 3–1 Championship Series win over Rochester)

John Kundla, *coach*

	Pos	Ht	Wt	College
Don Carlson	G	6–0	170	Minnesota
Jack Dwan	F-G	6–4	200	Loyola (Chicago)
Tony Jaros	F-G	6–3	185	Minnesota
Johnny Jorgensen	G-F	6–2	185	DePaul
George Mikan	C	6–10	245	DePaul
Paul Napolitano	F-G	6–2	185	San Francisco
Jim Pollard	F	6–4	185	Stanford
Herm Schaefer	G	6–0	175	Indiana
Donald Smith	G-F	6–2	190	Minnesota

1948–49

52–18

(BAA champions; includes 2–0 first- and second-round playoff wins over Chicago and Rochester and 4–2 Finals win over Washington)

John Kundla, *coach*

	Pos	Ht	Wt	College
Mike Bloom	F	6–6	190	Temple
Don Carlson	G	6–0	170	Minnesota
Jack Dwan	F-G	6–4	200	Loyola (Chicago)
Ray Ellefson	C	6–8	230	W. Texas State
Arnie Ferrin	F-G	6–2	180	Utah
Donnie Forman	G	5–10	175	NYU
Earl Gardner	F	6–3	195	DePauw
Tony Jaros	F-G	6–3	185	Minnesota
Johnny Jorgensen	G-F	6–2	185	DePaul
Whitey Kachan	G	6–2	185	DePaul
George Mikan	C	6–10	245	DePaul
Jim Pollard	F	6–4	185	Stanford
Herm Schaefer	G	6–0	175	Indiana
Donald Smith	G-F	6–2	190	Minnesota
Jack Tingle	F	6–4	205	Kentucky

1949–50

61–19

(NBA champions; includes 2–0 first-, second-, and third-round wins over Chicago, Ft. Wayne, and Anderson (Ind.), and 4–2 Finals win over Syracuse)

John Kundla, *coach*

	Pos	Ht	Wt	College
Don Carlson	G	6–0	170	Minnesota
Arnie Ferrin	F-G	6–2	180	Utah
Normie Glick	F	6–7	190	Loyola Marymount
Bud Grant	F	6–3	195	Minnesota
Bob Harrison	G	6–1	190	Michigan
Billy Hassett	G	5–11	180	Notre Dame
Tony Jaros	F-G	6–3	185	Minnesota
Slater Martin	G	5–10	170	Texas
George Mikan	C	6–10	245	DePaul
Vern Mikkelsen	F-C	6–7	230	Hamline
Jim Pollard	F	6–4	185	Stanford
Herm Schaefer	G	6–0	175	Indiana
Gene Stump	F-G	6–2	185	DePaul
Lefty Walther	G	6–2	160	Tennessee

1951–52

49–30

(NBA champions; includes 2–0 first-round win over Indianapolis, 3–1 second-round win over Rochester, and 4–3 Finals win over New York)

John Kundla, ***coach***

	Pos	Ht	Wt	College
Bob Harrison	G	6–1	190	Michigan
Lew Hitch	F-C	6–8	200	Kansas State
Joe Hutton	G	6–1	170	Hamline
Slater Martin	G	5–10	170	Texas
George Mikan	C	6–10	245	DePaul
Vern Mikkelsen	F-C	6–7	230	Hamline
John Pilch	F	6–3	185	Wyoming
Jim Pollard	F	6–4	185	Stanford
Pep Saul	G-F	6–2	185	Seton Hall
Howie Schultz	C-F	6–6	200	Hamline
Whitey Skoog	G	5–11	180	Minnesota

1952–53

57–25

(NBA champions; includes 2–0 first-round win over Indianapolis, 3–2 second-round win over Ft. Wayne, and 4–1 Finals win over New York)

John Kundla, *coach*

	Pos	Ht	Wt	College
Bob Harrison	G	6–1	190	Michigan
Lew Hitch	F-C	6–8	200	Kansas State
Jim Holstein	F-G	6–3	180	Cincinnati
Slater Martin	G	5–10	170	Texas
George Mikan	C	6–10	245	DePaul
Vern Mikkelsen	F-C	6–7	230	Hamline
Jim Pollard	F	6–4	185	Stanford
Pep Saul	G-F	6–2	185	Seton Hall
Howie Schultz	C-F	6–6	200	Hamline
Whitey Skoog	G	5–11	180	Minnesota

1953–54

55–30

(NBA champions; includes opening round-robin wins over Rochester (109–88) and Ft. Wayne (twice: 90–85, 78–73); 2–1 Western Division finals win over Rochester; and 4–3 championship finals win over Syracuse)

John Kundla, *coach*

	Pos	Ht	Wt	College
Jim Holstein	F-G	6–3	180	Cincinnati
Clyde Lovellette	C-F	6–9	234	Kansas
Slater Martin	G	5–10	170	Texas
George Mikan	C	6–10	245	DePaul
Vern Mikkelsen	F-C	6–7	230	Hamline
Jim Pollard	F	6–4	185	Stanford
Pep Saul	G-F	6–2	185	Seton Hall
Dick Schnittker	F	6–5	200	Ohio State
Whitey Skoog	G	5–11	180	Minnesota

1971–72

81–16

(NBA champions; includes 4–0 first round win over Chicago, 4–2 second-round win over Milwaukee; and 4–1 Finals win over New York)

Bill Sharman, *coach*

	Pos	Ht	Wt	College
Elgin Baylor	F	6–5	225	Seattle
Wilt Chamberlain	C	7–1	250	Kansas
Jim Cleamons	G	6–3	185	Ohio State
Leroy Ellis	C-F	6–10	210	St. John's
Keith Erickson	F-G	6–5	195	UCLA
Gail Goodrich	G	6–1	170	UCLA
Happy Hairston	F	6–7	225	NYU
Jim McMillian	F	6–5	215	Columbia
Pat Riley	G-F	6–4	205	Kentucky
Flynn Robinson	G	6–1	185	Wyoming
John Trapp	F	6–7	210	Nevada-Las Vegas
Jerry West	G	6–2	175	West Virginia

1979–80

72–26

(NBA champions; includes 4–1 first round win over Phoenix, 4–1 second-round win over Seattle; and 4–2 Finals win over Philadelphia)

Jack McKinney, Paul Westhead, *coaches*

	Pos	Ht	Wt	College
Kareem Abdul-Jabbar	C	7–2	225	UCLA
Ron Boone	G-F	6–2	200	Idaho State
Marty Byrnes	F	6–7	215	Syracuse
Kenny Carr	F	6–7	220	N.C. State
Jim Chones	C-F	6–11	220	Marquette
Michael Cooper	G-F	6–5	170	New Mexico
Don Ford	F	6–9	215	Cal-Santa Barbara
Spencer Haywood	F-C	6–8	225	Detroit
Brad Holland	G	6–3	180	UCLA
Magic Johnson	G	6–8	215	Michigan State
Mark Landsberger	F-C	6–8	215	Arizona State
Butch Lee	G	6–0	185	Marquette
Ollie Mack	G	6–3	185	East Carolina
Norm Nixon	G	6–2	170	Duquesne
Jamaal Wilkes	F-G	6–6	190	UCLA

1981–82

69–27

(NBA champions; includes 4–0 first round win over Phoenix, 4–0 second-round win over San Antonio; and 4–2 Finals win over Philadelphia)

Paul Westhead, Pat Riley, *coaches*

	Pos	Ht	Wt	College
Kareem Abdul-Jabbar	C	7–2	225	UCLA
Jim Brewer	F-C	6–9	210	Minnesota
Michael Cooper	G-F	6–5	170	New Mexico
Clay Johnson	G	6–4	175	Missouri
Eddie Jordan	G	6–1	170	Rutgers
Magic Johnson	G	6–8	215	Michigan State
Mitch Kupchak	F-C	6–9	230	North Carolina
Mark Landsberger	F-C	6–8	215	Arizona State
Bob McAdoo	C-F	6–9	210	North Carolina
Mike McGee	G-F	6–5	190	Michigan
Kevin McKenna	G-F	6–5	195	Creighton
Norm Nixon	G	6–2	170	Duquesne
Kurt Rambis	F	6–8	213	Santa Clara
Jamaal Wilkes	F-G	6–6	190	UCLA

1984–85

77–24

(NBA champions; includes 3–0 first round win over Phoenix, 4–1 Western Conference semifinals win over Portland, 4–1 Western Conference finals win over Denver, and 4–2 Finals win over Boston)

Pat Riley, *coach*

	Pos	Ht	Wt	College
Kareem Abdul-Jabbar	C	7–2	225	UCLA
Michael Cooper	G-F	6–5	170	New Mexico
Magic Johnson	G	6–8	215	Michigan State
Earl Jones	C	7–0	210	District of Columbia
Mitch Kupchak	F-C	6–9	230	North Carolina
Ronnie Lester	G	6–2	175	Iowa
Bob McAdoo	C-F	6–9	210	North Carolina
Mike McGee	G-F	6–5	190	Michigan
Chuck Nevitt	C	7–5	217	N.C. State
Kurt Rambis	F	6–8	213	Santa Clara
Byron Scott	G	6–3	195	Arizona State
Larry Spriggs	F	6–7	230	Howard
Jamaal Wilkes	F-G	6–6	190	UCLA
James Worthy	F	6–9	225	North Carolina

1986–87

80–20

(NBA champions; includes 3–0 first round win over Denver, 4–1 Western Conference semifinals win over Golden State, 4–0 Western Conference finals win over Seattle, and 4–2 Finals win over Boston)

Pat Riley, *coach*

	Pos	Ht	Wt	College
Kareem Abdul-Jabbar	C	7–2	225	UCLA
Adrian Branch	F-G	6–7	185	Maryland
Frank Brickowski	F-C	6–9	240	Penn State
Michael Cooper	G-F	6–5	170	New Mexico
A. C. Green	F-C	6–9	230	Oregon State
Magic Johnson	G	6–8	215	Michigan State
Wes Matthews	G	6–1	170	Wisconsin
Kurt Rambis	F	6–8	213	Santa Clara
Byron Scott	G	6–3	195	Arizona State
Mike Smrek	C	7–0	250	Canisius
Billy Thompson	F	6–7	195	Louisville
Mychal Thompson	C-F	6–10	226	Minnesota
James Worthy	F	6–9	225	North Carolina

1987–88

77–29

(NBA champions; includes 3–0 first round win over San Antonio, 4–3 Western Conference semifinals win over Utah, 4–3 Western Conference finals win over Dallas, and 4–3 Finals win over Detroit)

Pat Riley, *coach*

	Pos	Ht	Wt	College
Kareem Abdul-Jabbar	C	7–2	225	UCLA
Tony Campbell	F-G	6–7	215	Ohio State
Michael Cooper	G-F	6–5	170	New Mexico
A. C. Green	F-C	6–9	230	Oregon State
Magic Johnson	G	6–8	215	Michigan State
Jeff Lamp	F-G	6–6	195	Virginia
Wes Matthews	G	6–1	170	Wisconsin
Kurt Rambis	F	6–8	213	Santa Clara
Byron Scott	G	6–3	195	Arizona State
Mike Smrek	C	7–0	250	Canisius
Billy Thompson	F	6–7	195	Louisville
Mychal Thompson	C-F	6–10	226	Minnesota
Ray Tolbert	F	6–9	225	Indiana
Milt Wagner	G	6–5	185	Louisville
James Worthy	F	6–9	225	North Carolina

1999–2000

82–23

(NBA champions; includes 3–2 first round win over Sacramento, 4–1 Western Conference semifinals win over Phoenix, 4–3 Western Conference finals win over Portland, and 4–2 Finals win over Indiana)

Phil Jackson, *coach*

	Pos	Ht	Wt	College
Kobe Bryant	G	6–6	200	None
John Celestand	G	6–4	178	Villanova
Derek Fisher	G	6–1	200	Ark.-Little Rock
Rick Fox	G-F	6–7	230	North Carolina
Devean George	G-F	6–8	220	Augsburg
A. C. Green	F-C	6–9	230	Oregon State
Ron Harper	G-F	6–6	216	Miami (Ohio)
Robert Horry	F	6–9	220	Alabama
Sam Jacobson	G-F	6–4	215	Minnesota
Travis Knight	C	7–0	235	Connecticut
Tyronn Lue	G	6–0	175	Nebraska
Shaquille O'Neal	C	7–1	300	LSU
Glen Rice	F-G	6–7	215	Michigan
John Salley	F-C	6–11	230	Georgia Tech
Brian Shaw	G	6–6	190	Cal-Santa Barbara

2000–2001

71–27

(NBA champions; includes 3–0 first round win over Portland, 4–0 Western Conference semifinals win over Sacramento, 4–0 Western Conference finals win over San Antonio, and 4–1 Finals win over Philadelphia)

Phil Jackson, *coach*

	Pos	Ht	Wt	College
Kobe Bryant	G	6–6	200	None
Derek Fisher	G	6–1	200	Ark.-Little Rock
Greg Foster	F-C	6–11	240	Texas-El Paso
Rick Fox	G-F	6–7	230	North Carolina
Devean George	G-F	6–8	220	Augsburg
Horace Grant	F-C	6–10	215	Clemson
Ron Harper	G-F	6–6	216	Miami (Ohio)
Robert Horry	F	6–9	220	Alabama
Tyronn Lue	G	6–0	175	Nebraska
Mark Madsen	F	6–9	240	Stanford
Stanislav Medvedenko	F	6–10	250	Ukraine
Shaquille O'Neal	C	7–1	300	LSU
Mike Penberthy	G	6–3	185	Master's
Isaiah Rider	G-F	6–5	215	Nevada-Las Vegas
Brian Shaw	G	6–6	190	Cal-Santa Barbara

2001–2002

73–28

(NBA champions; includes 3–0 first round win over Portland, 4–1 Western Conference semifinals win over San Antonio, 4–3 Western Conference finals win over Sacramento, and 4–0 Finals win over New Jersey)

Phil Jackson, *coach*

	Pos	Ht	Wt	College
Kobe Bryant	G	6–6	200	None
Joe Crispin	G	6–0	185	Penn State
Derek Fisher	G	6–1	200	Ark.-Little Rock
Rick Fox	G-F	6–7	230	North Carolina
Devean George	G-F	6–8	220	Augsburg
Robert Horry	F	6–9	220	Alabama
Lindsey Hunter	G	6–2	170	Jackson State
Mark Madsen	F	6–9	240	Stanford
Jelani McCoy	C	6–10	245	UCLA
Stanislav Medvedenko	F	6–10	250	Ukraine
Shaquille O'Neal	C	7–1	300	LSU
Mike Penberthy	G	6–3	185	Master's
Mitch Richmond	G	6–5	215	Kansas State
Brian Shaw	G	6–6	190	Cal-Santa Barbara
Samaki Walker	F	6–9	240	Louisville

BIBLIOGRAPHY

Bucher, Ric. "I 2 I." *ESPN the Magazine*, Nov. 7, 2005: 79.

Cobourn, R. Thomas. *Kareem Abdul-Jabbar*. New York: Chelsea House Publishers, 1995.

Christgau, John. *Tricksters in the Madhouse: Lakers vs. Globetrotters, 1948*. Lincoln, Neb.: University of Nebraska Press, 2004.

Devaney, John. *Where Are They Now? Great Sports Stars of Yesteryear*. New York: Crown Publishers, Inc., 1985.

Heisler, Mark. *The Lives of Riley*. New York: Macmillan, 1994.

Heisler, Mark. *Madmen's Ball: The Inside Story of the Lakers' Dysfunctional Dynasties*. Chicago: Triumph Books, 2004.

Jackson, Phil with Michael Arkush. *The Last Season: A Team in Search of Its Soul*. New York: The Penguin Press, 2004.

Johnson Jr., Earvin "Magic" and Roy S. Johnson. *Magic's Touch*. Reading, Mass.: Addison-Wesley Publishing Company, Inc. 1989.

Kawakami, Tim with Scott Howard-Cooper. *Laker Glory: The 2000 NBA Champions*. Los Angeles: Los Angeles Times Books, 2000.

Kaye, Elizabeth. *Ain't No Tomorrow: Kobe, Shaq, and the Making of a Lakers Dynasty*. Chicago: Contemporary Books, 2002.

Lazenby, Roland. *The Lakers: A Basketball Journey*. New York: St. Martin's Press, 1993.

Lazenby, Roland. *The Show: The Inside Story of the Spectacular Los Angeles Lakers in the Words of Those Who Lived It*. New York: McGraw-Hill, 2006.

Libby, Bill. *We Love You Lakers*. New York: SPORT Magazine Press, 1972.

Ostler, Scott and Steve Springer. *Winnin' Times: The Magical Journey of the Los Angeles Lakers*. New York: Macmillan Publishing Company, 1986.

Rosen, Charley. *The Pivotal Season: How the 1971–72 Los Angeles Lakers Changed the NBA*. New York: Thomas Dunne Books, 2005.

Rubenstein, Barry. "Have Fun, Drink Pepsi, Wear Reebok (And Let Michael Win NBA Championships)" *Athlon Sports 1996–97 Pro Basketball Edition*. Nashville: Athlon Sports Communications, Inc., 1996.

Rubenstein, Barry and Lyle Spencer. *The BIG Title: NBA 2000 Champion Los Angeles Lakers, the Official NBA Finals 2000 Retrospective*. New York: Broadway Books, 2000.

Rupprecht, Josh and Ryan Thompson, John Black. *2005–06 Los Angeles Lakers Media Guide*. Los Angeles Lakers, 2005.

Sharpe, Wilton. *Wildcat Madness: Great Eras in Kentucky Basketball*. Nashville, TN: Cumberland House Publishing, 2005.

Shouler, Ken and Bob Ryan, Sam Smith, Leonard Koppett, Bob Bellotti. *TOTAL Basketball: The Ultimate Basketball Encyclopedia*. Toronto, Ontario, Canada: Sport Media Publishing, Inc., 2003.

Springer, Steve. *The Los Angeles Times Encyclopedia of the Lakers*. Los Angeles: The Los Angeles Times, 1998.

Thornley, Stew. *The History of the Lakers: Basketball's Original Dynasty*. Minneapolis, Minn.: Nodin Press, 1989.

WEB SITES:

Associated Press. "Basketball Legend George Mikan Dies." Foxnews.com. http://www.foxnews.com/story/0,2933,158428,00.html, June 2, 2005.

Associated Press. "Kobe's 81-point game second only to Wilt." http://sports.espn.go.com/nba/recap?gameId=260122013, Jan. 22, 2006.

Associated Press. "Kobe scores 27 as Lakers pull away late against Blazers." SportingNews.com. http://sports.espn.go.com/nba/recap?gameId=260221013, Feb. 21, 2006.

Associated Press. "Lakers lead Kings wire to wire, take seventh in West." http://sports.espn.go.com/nba/recap?gameId=260322013, March 22, 2006.

Associated Press. "Kobe scores 50, sets Lakers' season scoring mark." http://sports.espn.go.com/nba/recap?gameId=260414013, April 15, 2006.

Associated Press. "Bryant's bucket at buzzer pushes Suns to edge of elimination." http://sports.espn.go.com/nba/recap?gameId=260430013, April 30, 2006

Beacham, Greg. "LA Lakers 106, Golden State 94." http://sports.yahoo.com/nba/recap?gid=2006030309&prov=ap, March 4, 2006.

Jackson, Scoop. "It Has Happened—Must-See Kobe." ESPN.com, Page 2. http://sports.espn.go.com/espn/page2/story?page=jackson/060124, Jan. 24, 2006.

NBA.com. "Commissioner Stern, NBA Greats Pay Tribute to Mikan." http://www.nba.com/news/nba_statement_mikan_050602.html, June 3, 2005.

NBA Encyclopedia Playoff Edition. "1999–2000 Season in Review: Lakers Shaq-le NBA." nba.com. http://www.nba.com/history/season/19992000.

Simmons, Bill. "Who's the NBA MVP?" ESPN.com, Page 2. http://sports.espn.go.com/espn/page2/story?page=simmons/060414, April 14, 2006.

SportsTicker. "Wallace, Bowen headline first team all-defensive team." http://sports.espn.go.com/nba/news/story?id=2441608, May 11, 2006.

www.basketball-reference.com/

INDEX

www.ingramcontent.com/pod-product-compliance
Lightning Source LLC
Jackson TN
JSHW020017141224
75386JS00025B/566

9781581825541